Rum, Slaves
and Molasses

OTHER BOOKS BY
CLIFFORD LINDSEY ALDERMAN

The Rhode Island Colony

The Royal Opposition:
   The Story of the British Generals in
   the American Revolution

Clifford Lindsey Alderman

Rum, Slaves and Molasses

The Story of New England's Triangular Trade

CROWELL-COLLIER PRESS • New York, New York

For Nancy Lucas, an aspiring young author,
with best wishes for her success

The Macmillan Company, 866 Third Avenue, New York, N.Y. 10022
Collier-Macmillan Canada Ltd., Toronto, Ontario
Library of Congress catalog card number: 70-188772
Printed in the United States of America

10 9 8 7 6 5 4 3 2 1

Map by Rafael Palacios

PICTURE CREDITS (picture insert follows page 40): Brown Brothers,
viii (top); Historical Pictures Service, Chicago, iii, iv (bottom), vi,
vii (top); The New-York Historical Society, New York City, i; Ken-
neth M. Newman, Old Print Shop, New York City, viii (bottom);
Radio Times Hulton Picture Library, ii, iv (top), v, vii (bottom).

Contents

UNITED STATES

KENTUCKY

TENNESSEE

WEST FLA.

GEORGIA

VIRGINIA

NORTH CAROLINA

S.C.

EAST FLA.

PA.

N.Y.

VT.

N.H.

CONN.

MASS.

R.I.

N.J.

DEL.

MD.

D.C.

Dover

Portsmouth

Salem

Boston

Providence

Bristol

Newport

New London

New Haven

ATLANTIC

BAHAMA ISLANDS

Havana

CUBA

JAMAICA

HAITI

SANTO DOMINGO

HISPANIOLA

GREATER ANTILLES

PUERTO RICO

ST. CHRISTOPHER

NEVIS

LESSER ANTILLES

VIRGIN ISLANDS

ST. THOMAS

ST. JOHN

ST. CROIX

ANTIGUA

MARTINIQUE

BARBADOS

WEST INDIES

CARIBBEAN SEA

SOUTH AMERICA

ROUTE OF THE
SUKEY
1802

Miles

0   500   1000

map by palacios

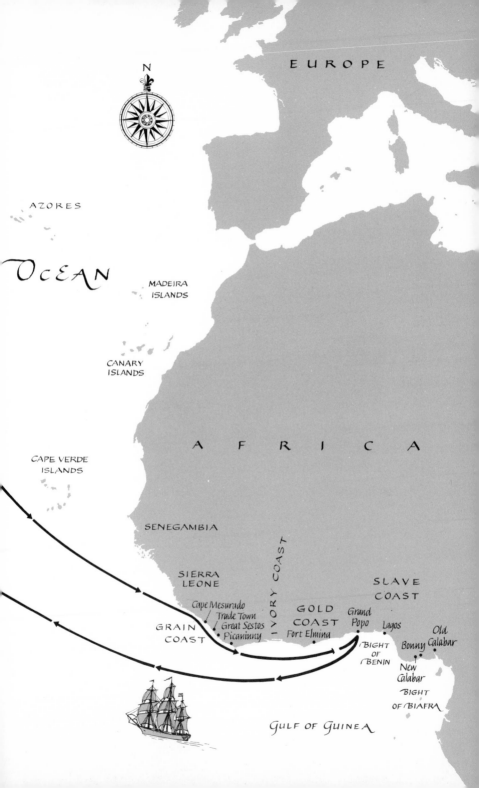

1.

The Sukey Sails

She lay alongside captain jim dewolf's wharf that day in 1802, a smart, trim topsail schooner, nearly ready for sea. On her stern was lettered her name, *Sukey,* and below it: Bristol, Rhode Island.

As usual, the Bristol waterfront buzzed with feverish activity that day, especially on Captain Jim's wharf. Heavy ox carts laden with last minute cargo lumbered slowly over the cobblestones of Thames Street that edged the wharf, and then onto it.

Captain Jim and some of his brothers owned the carts and oxen, the distillery on Thames Street from which most of the *Sukey's* outward cargo had come and the countinghouse that was the headquarters for their business. In the West Indies, or Sugar Islands, as they were often called in those days, the deWolfs owned plantations to provide the cargo the *Sukey* would bring back to Bristol on the homeward part of her long voyage. And they owned the *Sukey* and other ships that sailed in the evil trade in which they were engaged.

The carts were bringing the last of the rum from the distillery. When they had rattled onto the wharf, hoisting devices called windlasses creaked and groaned as the big hogsheads were lifted, swung aboard and lowered into the bilge, the lowest part of the schooner, just above her keel. One reason heavy cargo was stowed deep was that it helped a vessel to ride easily at sea. The bilge was already so crammed with hogsheads that it seemed impossible to find room for more, but they did, and soon this lower hold was loaded "chockablock," as seafaring men called it.

There were a few more packages, bales and cases yet to go aboard. They went into the 'tween decks, along with the rest of the trade goods. Queer cargo the trade goods were—packaged bolts or rolls of scarlet broadcloth, a case of glossy silk material called lutestring, twenty-four dozen men's hats in colors of red, green and white, embroidered with tinsel lace, three thousand knives with yellow handles, and a miscellaneous lot of necklaces, rings, snuff, cigars and muskets.

The 'tween decks, six feet high, made up the next level above the bilge. It did not run the whole length of the ship, for space had to be left for the hatches leading to the bilge, for the cabin—the officers' quarters—at the stern or rear end of the ship and for the forecastle (sailors call it the foc's'le), where the crew lived, at the forward end. Once the *Sukey* reached the Guinea Coast of West Africa and the trade goods were disposed of, the 'tween decks would be used for an entirely different purpose.

Provisions for the voyage to Africa and casks or butts of fresh water also went aboard, as well as a large number of wooden planks. On the schooner's manifest it said the planks were for repairs to the ship. It seemed as if they must expect a lot of damage during the voyage, though the *Sukey* was staunch and seaworthy.

The truth was that the planks were not for repairs. The use that would be made of them was a terrible and sinister one. If it had been set down on the manifest, the *Sukey* could not have been given clearance to sail, and her owners would have been liable for arrest and heavy fines. But since it was not, there was no evidence that the law passed in 1787 by the Rhode Island State Assembly, strictly forbidding the trade in which the *Sukey* was engaged, was being broken, though everybody knew perfectly well that it was.

The *Sukey*, however, had no trouble getting her

clearance papers after an inspection by the Bristol surveyor. Her trade and that of many another Bristol vessel brought too much prosperity to too many people. There were the Bristol sailmakers and carpenters, the caulkers who sealed the wooden ships' joints with oakum and tar, the ship chandlers who sold provisions and an endless variety of wares needed aboard a vessel, and the owners and workers of the ropewalks that made cordage—the great number of ropes used in holding, hoisting, lowering and controlling the sails of a ship. And there were many more who depended upon the Bristol shipowners for profit and wages.

Any seafaring man could tell at a glance, from the sharp lines of her hull and the large spread of canvas her two masts could carry, that the *Sukey* was built for speed and easy handling at sea. She and other vessels in her trade needed that. The New England coastal waters and the Caribbean Sea, which she would reach in time, were infested with pirates—the hijackers of those days.

If she could not outrun a pirate, the *Sukey* was prepared to fight. On the main deck—the topmost one, also called the weather deck because it was open to wind and weather—were lashed two carronades—short, stubby cannon about four feet long that fired heavy balls. At her stern was a smaller brass cannon, called a chaser, for firing at a ship overtaking from astern.

And in her cabin was a chest of small arms— muskets and pistols—to be used if pirates tried or managed to get aboard the ship. They could also be used if the vessel's crew mutinied against the captain, or master, as he was also called. And they could be used against the "cargo" the *Sukey* would take aboard on the Guinea Coast.

Also in the cabin was the medicine chest. Most of the medicine was made from Peruvian bark, which later became the source of quinine, the common remedy for malaria and other tropical fevers. The bark medicine was going to be needed along the swampy, fever-ridden Guinea Coast.

The *Sukey,* only seventy feet long, was too small to carry a doctor—or surgeon, as he is always called aboard ships, though he does not often perform an operation at sea. Captain Jacob Almy would handle the surgeon's job. Of course, he was not a regular doctor. There is a yarn about the master of a sailing ship in the old days and a sailor who fell ill. The captain examined the man and then consulted the directions in the medicine chest. The bottles of medicine were numbered, and the sailor's symptoms called for a dose from the one numbered nine. Alas, bottle No. 9 was empty. So the skipper mixed equal parts of medicine from bottle No. 4 and bottle No. 5 and dosed the poor fellow with it. The story does not tell whether he recovered.

Babbitt's wharf, next to deWolf's, was a good place from which to view the *Sukey's* trimness. On that day in 1802, Babbitt's wharf probably was as busy as its neighbor. If a vessel from the Sugar Islands was discharging her cargo, there would be, in addition to the usual hubbub of unloading, a rabble of boys clustered about the hogsheads already landed on the wharf and chanting:

Mister Babbitt,
Lemme labbit.

Mister Babbitt let them labbit. The boys carried slivers of shingle. They would dip them into the bunghole of a hogshead or, spotting a leaky cask the cooper had not gotten around to sealing, they would scrape the little pieces of wood over the dark, sticky liquid that oozed out and lick it off. This was called labbing, and most Bristol wharf-owners let the boys have their taste of the sweet molasses.

Yes, Babbitt's wharf was a good place from which to see the *Sukey*. There, all you noticed about the air around you was the sweet odor of molasses and the heavy, sickish-sweet smell of rum from the distilleries.

But on deWolf's wharf that day, when you came close enough to the schooner, there was another smell—a smell that seemed to make your very insides curl up. It was a smell so vile and horrible that you wondered how the *Sukey*'s crew could possibly stand it.

"You can smell a slaver five miles downwind," they said on the Guinea Coast. And the *Sukey* was a slaver.

True, her 'tween decks had been thoroughly scrubbed with vinegar to purify them. In those times the powerful disinfectants used today were unknown, and vinegar was supposed to have antiseptic properties. Aboard slave ships its sharp tang at least helped to make the smell a little better, though it didn't do much to disinfect a vessel. And the molasses the *Sukey* had brought from the West Indies sweetened the air a little.

Yet the smell clung. It would always be there. After the *Sukey* left the Guinea Coast with her "cargo," it would be so frightful that it cannot be described.

When the last of the schooner's cargo was aboard, three men marched onto the wharf from the direction of the countinghouse. One was Captain James deWolf. He was the richest of the five deWolf brothers and a sailorman to the core. He had a florid complexion, snub nose, gray eyes with the seafaring man's farseeing look, and big, strong sailor's hands.

Beside him strode Captain Almy, of whom there is no description in the records, and the pilot, Nathaniel Ingraham. The *Sukey* was going to need Ingraham to reach the open sea.

Bristol lies at the upper end of Narragansett Bay. To reach the Atlantic, the *Sukey* must sail through the narrow East Passage, between big Aquidneck and the two smaller islands of Prudence and Conanicut. Nathaniel Ingraham, after years of sailing small coasting vessels in Narragansett Bay, knew every shoal and sand bar of the narrow strait and would be paid six dollars for guiding the *Sukey* through it.

Captain Almy carried a packet containing the *Sukey's* documents—manifest, clearance papers, the bill of health for which Captain Jim had paid $5.46 at the Bristol customs house and the instructions that told him in great detail just what he was to do on the *Sukey's* long voyage. Much would be left to Almy's own judgment, however, for slavers always faced perils of the sea, unexpected delays, disease, attack by pirates and many other situations that could not possibly be foreseen.

At the gangway, Captain Jim shook hands with

Captain Almy and wished him Godspeed and a prosperous and speedy voyage. It was no gesture of deep friendship. DeWolf was thinking of the money that would come flooding into the coffers of his countinghouse at the end of a successful voyage.

The crew was already aboard. Just how many the *Sukey* carried is not known. In addition to the captain there would be two mates in a vessel of this size, a carpenter, possibly a quartermaster or supercargo to attend to the vessel's accounts and perhaps some of the trading in Africa and the West Indies, a cooper to repair leaky hogsheads, a cook, perhaps half a dozen sailors—hands before the mast —and a ship's boy to look after the captain's and mates' quarters.

Some of the sailors were little more than boys. Rhode Island was rivaled only by Massachusetts as a seafaring state, and many of its inhabitants were seafaring people, bred to the sea and ships. But few wanted to sail aboard a Bristol slaver. The voyage was the most perilous of all in which New England ships engaged. To ship out in a slaver, a young fellow needed two things: a spirit of adventure to make him forget the dangers, and a very strong stomach.

The pay wasn't much. Captain Almy got thirty

dollars a month, and the lowest-paid of all the *Sukey*'s crew—the ship's boy, Elkanah Waldron—got eight dollars. Still, money was worth far more then than today. And the captain, the mates and the crew had the right to do small amounts of trading on their own. On the Guinea Coast or in the West Indies a dozen knives from Pardon Handy's ship chandlery in Bristol could be traded for all sorts of things—parrots, birds of paradise, monkeys, cases of tropical fruit or West Indian cigars. Back in Bristol—provided the *Sukey* did get back—these could be sold for a nice profit.

Now it was sailing time. Captain Almy and the mates barked orders that the crew scurried to obey. Whether the skipper had visited an astrologer earlier is not known, but many a New England slaver captain did. Astrologers in seaport towns did a thriving business, preparing astrological charts showing the exact day, hour and minute a vessel must sail for a successful voyage.

At any rate, the *Sukey*'s lines were being cast off. Blocks and tackles groaned and squeaked as the schooner "made sail" by hoisting and setting her canvas. Regular schooners were rigged with roughly triangular fore-and-aft sails—that is, sails that run in a lengthwise direction. The *Sukey*, being a topsail schooner, would have had a square-rigged topsail (pronounced "tops'l") above the fore-and-aft sail on her first or foremast ("forem'st") and probably another called a topgallantsail ("to'g'ants'l") above that. The normal position of a square sail was athwartships—at right angles to the ship's length. But all sails could be trimmed—set to catch the wind in the best way—by swinging them in one direction or another.

Schooners also carried smaller triangular sails called spritsails ("sprits'ls") and jibs, fastened to the pole called the jib boom and its extension, the bowsprit, that reached out ahead of the bow.

Probably a fair-sized crowd of the crew's families and friends were gathered on deWolf's wharf as the *Sukey* sheered gently away, already feeling the drive of the wind that must carry her to the Guinea Coast. She moved slowly down the harbor like a white-winged bird skimming over the blue water and sparkling whitecaps.

People on the wharf cried, "Huzza!" and waved their hats. The *Sukey* was off on her voyage. In West Africa she would work her way down the Guinea Coast, probably finding it necessary to stop at port after port as she exchanged her trade goods and precious rum for even more precious black slaves, and perhaps also for gold dust, ivory, ebony and other African products.

At last she would head west, crossing the Atlantic over the infamous Middle Passage to the West Indies. In the islands the slaves would be landed and sold. Then Captain Almy would fill the *Sukey* chockablock with hogsheads of molasses to be distilled into more rum in Bristol.

This was the evil, cruel business known as the Triangular, or Three-Cornered, Trade. It was the cornerstone of much of New England's prosperity in the eighteenth and early nineteenth centuries. It made many men rich, but it was a part of what was to bring disgrace upon white men, misery and oppression upon black people and untold trouble upon the world.

2.

How It Began

SLAVERY IS AS OLD AS THE EARLIEST RECORDS OF history, and probably even older. Every race, at one time or another, has had slaves. Slaves were used to build the famous pyramids of Egypt, which took nearly two thousand years, from about 4750 to 3000 B.C. The ancient Romans captured and enslaved many thousands of their enemies during their conquest of all the Mediterranean, most of Europe and part of Asia. The ancient Greeks had slaves.

So did the warlike Carib Indians, who inhabited the long chain of small West Indian islands called today the Windward and Leeward groups of the Lesser Antilles. They often raided the four big islands of the Greater Antilles—today Puerto Rico, Hispaniola (Haiti and the Dominican Republic), Cuba and Jamaica—where the Arawak Indians lived.

The Caribs were cannibals; the name Carib (from which comes the name of the Caribbean Sea, where all the West Indies lie) is itself like the Spanish word *caribe,* meaning cannibal. Arawak men captured by the Caribs were roasted and eaten; the women and children were kept as slaves.

But the real curse of slavery that came to the West Indies lay in the African slave trade. It began as a result of the explorations of one of the most famous men in history.

Christopher Columbus is honored as the man who discovered the New World, though he was probably not the first explorer to land on its shores. Not as many people know that he was indirectly responsible for the beginning of the slave trade in the New World.

On October 12, 1492, Columbus landed on San Salvador, or Watlings Island, one of the many islands and cays of the Bahamas, off the eastern coast of Florida. On this first voyage, he also discovered the large islands of Cuba and Hispaniola. One of his three caravels, the *Santa Maria,* was wrecked on the shores of what is now Haiti. Largely from her timbers a fort was built called La Navidad, the Spanish name for Christmas, since it was then December. Columbus called the island *La Isla Española* (Spanish Island), but in time its inhabitants took to pronouncing it Hispaniola.

The explorer picked thirty-nine men to stay and man the fort, promising to return after he had delivered the sensational news to his benefactors, King Ferdinand and Queen Isabella of Spain, that he had discovered—so he thought—a new and shorter route to the East Indies.

The following year, when Columbus reached the fort on his second voyage of discovery, he found that La Navidad had been destroyed by the Indians (he naturally called them Indians since he thought he was in the East Indies). He ordered a strongly fortified town built somewhat farther east, to be called Isabella in honor of his benefactress. Leaving his brother Diego in command of the town, he went in search of gold on other islands.

In 1495 the Indians of Hispaniola decided that the white invaders of their island must be destroyed. They marched on the little settlement, but Diego sent two hundred foot soldiers, twenty horsemen and twenty savage dogs against them. Most of the Arawaks were killed, and those who survived were enslaved and put to work in the mines where the whites wrongly expected to find gold and silver.

The Arawaks were a proud race who fiercely loved freedom. In captivity many died. The settlers soon realized that it was not worthwhile keeping them as slaves. Then who was to do the hard work in the steamy tropical climate?

The Portuguese had already found an answer to much the same problem. They possessed four groups of islands in the Atlantic—the Cape Verdes, Madeiras and Canaries, not far off the West African coast, and the Azores, farther west. On all of them sugar cane was grown.

More than fifty years earlier, the Portuguese had penetrated Africa and reached its western coast. Along the shore of the Gulf of Guinea they had founded Lagos, today the capital of the Federation of Nigeria.

West Africa was a treasure-trove for traders. It had much gold, as well as ivory, ostrich plumes, pepper and, most valuable of all, people—black people who could be enslaved and made to work for the profit of their masters.

Sometime between 1440 and 1450 the Portuguese began trading in slaves at Lagos. Some were sent to Portugal itself, others to the Portuguese islands, where they were put to work growing and harvesting sugar cane and making it into sugar and molasses.

Christopher Columbus is believed to have brought sugar cane to Hispaniola on his second voyage. As more and more of the West Indies were colonized by Europeans, the growing of sugar cane spread throughout the chain of islands, for the soil and climate were ideal for it. In 1530 a Portuguese ship brought a cargo of slaves from Africa to the part of Hispaniola that is now Santo Domingo. It would be more than a century before the first slaves were brought to Virginia, but in that period cargo after cargo of them was shipped from Africa to the West Indies.

The Portuguese had built forts all along the Guinea Coast of West Africa so that they might keep the rich trade for themselves. The first one, Elmina, was begun in 1481. It was on the Gold Coast, today the Republic of Ghana, on the northern edge of the Gulf of Guinea. Its walls were thirty feet thick, with towers along them for defense, mounted with four hundred cannon. On the fort's land side were two deep ditches, or moats, cut out of solid rock. Inside, below the part of the fort used as a trading station, were dungeons that could hold a thousand slaves.

But even powerful Elmina and the rest of the chain of forts could not keep other European traders out as the fame of the fabulous west coast of Africa spread. By the middle of the sixteenth century, English, French, Dutch, Prussian, Danish and, for a time, Swedish traders came in. They too built forts for trading posts along the two-thousand-mile stretch of the Guinea Coast and squabbled over which parts of the coast would be their own trading territory. Sometimes traders of one country would buy a fort belonging to those of another; sometimes the forts changed hands in bloody battles.

By 1540, nearly three-quarters of a century before the American colonies began to be settled, ten thousand black slaves a year were being shipped from West Africa to the West Indies; still others were sold in Mexico and South America. By the time the seventeenth century began, it was estimated that nine hundred thousand slaves had been brought into these regions. And the Indians—Arawaks, Caribs and members of other tribes—had to a large extent been destroyed, since they could not survive enslavement.

Some of the American colonies, once they were fairly well settled, joined in this profitable slave trade. The New England colonies, especially Massachusetts and Rhode Island, had relied upon fishing and sea trade for much of their revenue.

At first most of this sea trade was either with other American colonies or the West Indies. The Caribbean islands bought dried fish, beef, pork, flour, bread, lumber and products made of wood, particularly the staves, hoops and heads from which hogsheads could be made for molasses. In the Caribbean, New England ships loaded molasses and crude brown sugar, as well as logwood, used in making a red dye, and tropical fruit to sell in the colonies.

Then the slave trade began. Even before cotton became the chief product of the American colonies in the deep south, Maryland and Virginia needed slaves to work in the tobacco fields under the hot summer sun. A great many of the slaves in these colonies were brought from the West Indies, although others came directly from Africa. There were also many slaves in the northern colonies.

The first American slave ship shown in the records was the *Rainbow,* which sailed from Boston for Africa in 1645. On the Guinea Coast her captain found a shortage of slaves at the trading posts. With the help of the captains of several English ships also waiting in vain for slaves, an expedition was organized to go into the interior. The slave hunters took along a "murderer," a light cannon also called a swivel gun because it was mounted so that it could easily be swung in any direction. With it they attacked a native village, killed many of its people and managed to capture a few slaves.

The *Rainbow*'s captain got only two for his share, but with this meager cargo he sailed back to Boston, since there was a good market for slaves there.

In Boston his troubles continued. The ship's owners learned that the raid on the African village had taken place on a Sunday. In the eyes of the stern Puritans, this was a shocking crime, and the captain was arrested and tried for murder, man-stealing and Sabbath-breaking. He was acquitted, however, since the Massachusetts Bay court decided it had no power to punish a man for something that happened outside the colony. The two slaves were seized by the government and sent home to Africa, so this first American slaving voyage on record was a dismal failure.

It was not until the first half of the eighteenth century that some New England merchants had a bright idea that promised great riches. New England needed industry. The first ironworks in America had been established at Saugus, Massachusetts, in 1644, and later iron ore was also being smelted in New Hampshire and Connecticut. But most of the tools, machinery for sawmills and gristmills, farming equipment and household utensils had to be imported from Europe.

Why not use the profitable West African slave trade to bring industry to New England? The plan was simple enough: build distilleries to turn molasses from the Sugar Islands into rum. Then ship the rum to West Africa, where it could be exchanged for slaves, who would then be taken to the West

Indies and sold. There new cargoes of molasses would be loaded for New England, where the distilleries would turn it into more rum for Africa.

Thus the Triangular, or Three-Cornered, Trade began: rum from New England to West Africa, slaves to the Sugar Islands, molasses home to the New England distilleries. Sometimes slaving was called the trade in "black ivory." The Triangular variety worked beautifully. In Africa slaves could be obtained easily and profitably in exchange for liquor. French brandy had been in the greatest demand there, but New England rum, produced at low cost and far better than that made in the Sugar Islands, just about put the brandy trade out of business. And the wretched, captive black people brought high prices in the Caribbean, where molasses was cheap.

By the 1760s Rhode Island had many distilleries, all working at top speed to turn out rum, chiefly for the slave trade, although New Englanders were fond of it too. They called it Kill-Devil or, even more appropriately, O-Be-Joyful. Massachusetts had more distill-houses, as they were called, but little Rhode Island was the chief slave trade colony in proportion to its size.

The Triangular Trade was thriving in both colonies, and to a much smaller extent in Connecticut

and probably New Hampshire. Merchant-ship owners were becoming fabulously rich and were in-
vesting much of their gains in other industries, such
as textile manufacturing and the making of spermaceti candles from whale oil. New England, formerly
dependent upon fishing, regular sea trade and farm
and forest products for its existence, was becoming
industrialized.

3.

The Guinea Coast

THE *Sukey*'s VOYAGE ALONG THE VAST STRETCH OF the Guinea Coast is by no means the whole story of the African part of the Triangular Trade. But since she is one of the few American slavers for which there are fairly complete records of a good part of her voyage, it will be well to follow her there as she disposes of her outward cargo loaded in Bristol and takes aboard her human one for the West Indies.

In fair weather, with a spanking breeze, the *Sukey* would bowl along under full sail at a good speed. While such a spell of fine weather lasted, the ship would almost sail herself, with only a helmsman on deck to keep her on course and the officer on watch, alert for signs of a change or any trouble. If the wind dropped to a full calm, the *Sukey* would have to lie dead in the water, though she would almost always drift slightly in one direction or another, carried by the currents that flow like rivers in most parts of the ocean.

Even if the weather was good, the wind sometimes blew so hard that the *Sukey* was in danger of capsizing. Then the sails had to be reefed. Above the boom to which the lower edges of the triangular sails were attached, pieces of rope were fastened in a line across the lower part of the sail, each with one of its ends dangling down loose. These ropes were known as reef points. They were also used on the square sails carried by many ships, fastened above the yards at the lower or upper edges of the sail. Reefing a sail was done by lowering the sail or raising its edge a little so that the first reef points could be wrapped around the boom, pulled tight and tied. In that way the sail would be made slightly smaller and better able to withstand the force of the wind.

If the wind blew even harder, another reef might be taken, using a second line of reef points higher up on the sail, and the sail made still smaller. Some sails had three or more lines of reef points. Thus the force of the wind on the sail could be reduced considerably if necessary.

Sometimes the wind would be so strong that a vessel had to "shorten sail" by "taking in," or furling, one or more of the sails altogether. In a full gale a ship occasionally had to ride out the storm "under bare poles," that is, with no sails at all. When the wind's direction changed even a little, the crew trimmed the sails to catch its full force and thus drive the ship ahead with all possible speed.

Meanwhile, the *Sukey's* carpenter (always, even today, called "Chips" in ships) was busy cutting those planks listed on the manifest into proper sizes for their real use. However, he would not be able to do anything more with them until the 'tween decks was cleared of the cargo stored there.

And so, gradually, the *Sukey* neared the coast of Africa. The first land sighted would have been the cluster of Portuguese islands called the Cape Verdes, a little over three hundred miles off the eastern-most point of the African continent, Cape Verde. Most slavers put in there to refill their water casks and often to lay in supplies of food, including some that would be fed to the slaves when they were loaded aboard.

Then the ships would go on to the African coast and begin the long, slow progress along the shore of the Gulf of Guinea. There stood many trading posts or "factories," as they were called, on the Grain Coast (today the Republic of Liberia), Ivory Coast (now the Ivory Coast Republic), Gold Coast (now Ghana) and the Slave Coast (including the modern republics of Togo, Dahomey and the Federation of Nigeria).

Captain Almy of the *Sukey* ran into bad luck. It often happened. Sometimes when a vessel put into a slave-trading post she would find eight or ten other ships waiting for human cargoes ahead of her. Sometimes there would be a shortage of the slaves who were brought to the factory from the interior of Africa. Sometimes it would be both. And haggling over prices with the manager, known as the factor, almost always took a long time.

It was five months before Captain Almy had his full cargo of one hundred and twenty slaves. During that time twenty-two of those he had loaded at Cape Mesurado on the Grain Coast, his first stop, had died and had to be replaced at other ports of call all the way down to the Slave Coast—Bassa, Trade Town, Great Sestos, Picaninny and Grand Popo.

Back in Bristol, Rhode Island, Captain Jim de-Wolf was not going to be pleased about all this. He had not expected the *Sukey*'s whole voyage from Bristol to West Africa to the Sugar Islands and home would last that long. Time was money. It would be that much longer before the *Sukey* could begin another voyage. And dead slaves meant his profits from the present one would be less.

Nevertheless, Captain Jim, long experienced as a slaver captain himself, would understand it was not Captain Almy's fault, though he might do a good deal of grumbling when the skipper got home. These delays and losses often happened, as will be seen later, and once in a while a ship would lose money on a voyage.

For the most part, the long sweep of the Gulf of Guinea's shoreline was beautiful. There were immense stretches of gleaming, white sandy beaches. Just back of them was the dense, bright green forest. Often mountains rose blue in the distance. But all this, as slavers well knew, was a sinister beauty. It concealed dangers and hardships hated and feared by officers and crews alike.

The first of the dangers was the surf. There were few trading stations where ships could come in close to shore unless a factory was up one of the mighty rivers that flow into the Gulf of Guinea. Usually, slave ships had to anchor well offshore. Farther in, the water was shallow, and tremendous waves rolled in on the beaches, breaking with a thunderous crash. Transportation of the cargo the vessel had brought and loading of the new one had to be done by small boats.

Kroomen, a tribe of black natives who lived on the Guinea Coast, did this job. They were all fishermen and boatmen, and their skill in handling their frail boats in the mountainous surf seemed miraculous. The roaring fury of the great rollers had no terrors for them, even though the canoes they used were long and narrow, with round bottoms, the easiest sort of craft to capsize, and with hulls only about an eighth of an inch thick.

The Kroomen used the canoes for transporting small loads of ebony, ivory and the much-prized camwood that was used to make a red dye. For the larger loads of slaves they had heavier, flat-bottomed craft. Either kind of boat, in the hands of less experienced men, would have quickly capsized or been swamped in the surf, and those aboard would have been drowned or been eaten by the hordes of sharks that always lurked in the Guinea Coast waters.

But the Kroomen—big, powerful fellows—never failed to get through. No doubt they would have made excellent slaves, but they did not worry about being kidnaped and shipped to the West Indies. They knew they were too valuable where they were.

As soon as the *Sukey* reached Cape Mesurado the crew hauled the trade goods out of the 'tween decks and stacked them on the main deck to wait the factor's arrival from the trading station. Meanwhile, the carpenter began installing in the 'tween decks the planks he had cut to size. He made two sets of platformlike shelves and placed one along each side of the ship, halfway between the floor of the 'tween decks and the underside of the main deck, six feet overhead. These platforms extended toward the middle of the vessel, with a space between them.

To the floors of the 'tween decks and the two platforms, the carpenter riveted double iron leg shackles, each with a padlock attached to it. When a slave was loaded into the 'tween decks with one leg shackled, he was cramped into a space five and a half feet long, a little less than three feet high, and about sixteen inches wide. On one side of him was another slave fastened to the same shackle. When the floor of the 'tween decks was filled, more slaves were put on the shelves above it.

On the main deck, the carpenter stretched a high netting along the side rails of the ship that are called bulwarks. He also put up a stout wooden barricade, with a gate that could be locked, to shut off the quarterdeck and cabin in the after end of the ship.

Not long after the *Sukey* had anchored, a canoe could be seen approaching from shore, now mounting the curling white crest of a giant roller, now disappearing into the trough between it and the next one. The black arms of the Kroomen paddlers, glistening with the palm oil they rubbed on their bodies, moved in a sure, perfect cadence that drove the flimsy little craft along swiftly.

In the calmer water alongside the *Sukey,* the factor climbed the Jacob's ladder of rope that had been lowered over the schooner's side.

Captain Almy, who doubtless already knew the factor well, gave him a hand over the bulwarks and a hearty welcome. Next he "dashed" the man he hoped would take some of his cargo in exchange for slaves. A dash was a kind of gift, a tip or bribe, usually a bottle of rum or perhaps a musket. Slaver captains never failed to dash a factor. Otherwise the trader might cheat the slaver or save his better slaves for the next ship. But dash or not, the captain always had to be shrewd and watchful.

When these formalities were over, the factor inspected the trade goods with the greatest care, determining which goods would be most popular with those who furnished his stock of slaves. Hogsheads of rum, he knew, were always in demand.

When the factor had examined everything, the Kroomen took him and the captain ashore through the booming surf to the factory. There, in the "palaver house" (palaver is a word used in West Africa to describe any kind of talk or argument), the real trading began.

If a trading post was fortified, like Fort Elmina

and other great establishments along the Guinea Coast, it was called a fort or castle; otherwise it was a factory. In the forts the factors were usually white men; in the factories, they might be either white or black. Captain Almy may have had instructions from Captain Jim to trade at the factories, for he appears to have avoided the big forts. It was usually easier to cheat a trader in charge of a smaller post.

However, a factory could be good-sized and comfortable, with a number of buildings. One factor wrote a description of a factory he established on the Guinea Coast. The palaver house, where he lived, was a two-story building with verandas running around the outside of both stories. On top was a lookout from which approaching ships could be spotted.

The factor's employees lived in the usual huts that natives—from kings or chiefs of tribes down to their own slaves—used for lodgings all over West Africa. The huts consisted of a circular wall of sun-baked mud, with a cone-shaped roof of bamboo cane thatched with grass. Other buildings included a storage house for trade goods, a separate kitchen and stockades called barracoons for the slaves who were brought from the interior. There was one barracoon for the men and one for the women, each consisting of a circle of pens, with an open space in the center where the slaves could exercise after their meals. At the gate of each barracoon was a cannon, and the slaves were constantly guarded by armed men. A tall fence of thickly planted hedge surrounded the entire factory.

At the smaller factories, the factor did not live in such comfort or have such extensive equipment. Most white factors were a poor lot, poorly paid, often fugitives from Europe because they had gotten into trouble there. Most of the time life was dull, with few pleasures. The heat and humidity were terrible and they lived in dread of tropical fevers like malaria and yellow fever, as well as dysentery and smallpox. Many factors took to drink and many died, either of disease or alcoholism.

Yet when it came to trading, a slaver's captain had to be sharp to cheat a factor, who knew all the tricks of the trade. That was why the exchange of goods and rum for slaves took so long. There was much palaver before a deal was made. Sometimes a captain and factor would haggle for weeks over the price to be paid for each slave.

The prices differed with the quality of the slaves the factor had. Natives of certain tribes were thought to make better slaves than others. Some were healthier and stronger, able to work harder and longer than others. Some made better domestic servants on the sugar plantations. Others were pre-

ferred because they were docile and would give
their masters in the West Indies no trouble.

Prices went up when there was a shortage of
slaves along the Guinea Coast. They were higher
too when a number of ships were anchored off a
factory or castle, all anxious to fill their holds as
soon as possible. Sometimes a factory's barracoons
would be empty and a captain would have to wait
until a caravan came out of the interior.

During all this time, while the slaver's captain
squatted on a grass mat in the palaver house, the
ship's crew generally had to remain aboard ship
with little or nothing to do. It was always an un-
comfortable time. On the Guinea Coast, there were
two seasons—the wet, from June to October, when
it rained continually, and the dry. There was little
to choose between them. In the dry season a hard-
driving wind called the harmattan raised great
choking clouds of yellow dust. Sometimes ships met
these yellow dust clouds as far as five hundred
miles from land. In the wet season the men had to
stay below decks most of the time, and always the air
was hot, humid and stifling.

If the palaver over a deal took a long time, the
crew sometimes mutinied. Often men fell ill of the
tropical diseases that were the most feared peril of
the coast, and some died.

But at last, when prices had been agreed upon,

the terrified slaves were brought out of the barracoons so the captain—and the surgeon if the slaver carried one—could inspect them and make a selection.

The slaves were stripped naked, and Captain Almy examined them with the greatest care. He felt their muscles, made them jump up and down and stretch their arms out and back rapidly. If a slave seemed out of breath he was instantly rejected. The condition of the teeth was most important; an old man or woman might be shaved so that no telltale gray hair showed, but decaying teeth were a sign of aging. There were other tricks that might fool even a factor, as one of them described. He was too smart, however, and he rejected a big, powerful-looking fellow when he learned the man had been given certain drugs to bloat him up, and others to make his skin look glossy and healthy.

Not being a doctor, Captain Almy had to use his own skill in detecting signs of smallpox or other diseases. Smallpox, yellow fever and other ills that spread easily were the most feared. One diseased slave might infect everyone aboard a ship and slaves who came down with such an illness at sea were almost always thrown overboard.

Each slave selected was branded with a red-hot

branding iron or wire so that a treacherous factor could not substitute another of poorer quality. The slaves Captain Almy bought were marked with Captain Jim's initials—JDW. Actually, the branding was not too painful, since the iron or wire was just hot enough when it was applied to blister but not seriously burn the slave's skin.

When the slaves Captain Almy selected had been branded they were marched in chains or handcuffs to the beach. More male slaves were bought than females, though some women were needed to produce children who could be raised to bring profit to a plantation owner at no additional cost to him.

Most of the captives had lived all their lives far in the interior, in the deep forests and jungles, the plains, hills or valleys. They had never seen the sea. Many thought the frightful crash of the surf was a great beast roaring, ready to devour them. One trader who wrote of his experiences in Africa said many slaves believed they were being taken to the land of a giant race of cannibals called Koomi, to be eaten. And no doubt many trembled at the sight of the horizon, that line where the sky and sea seemed to meet. Might the ship fall off there into some unknown, bottomless abyss?

Getting the slaves aboard a ship was often no easy task. Sometimes they struggled desperately against their guards. They would fling themselves on the sand, clutching handfuls of it in a vain effort to hang onto the land. Sometimes, once they were aboard the Kroomen's boats, they would manage to jump overboard, and were almost always drowned or seized and eaten by the sharks.

Meanwhile, the rum and other trade goods that had been bartered for the slaves had been taken ashore. The 'tween decks and the two platforms were ready for the human cargo. The blacks were stowed there much as if they had been so many logs, except for the cruel shackles. As each slave lay down, the padlock was snapped shut so that the iron held one leg fast.

When all had been loaded, the *Sukey* set sail for her next stop. If a slaver were lucky enough to obtain a full cargo at one factory or castle, she could head at once for the Middle Passage and the West Indies. This seldom happened, and filling a vessel with all the slaves that could be crammed into her usually required calls at several factories, as happened with the *Sukey*. The seven at which she stopped stretched over a distance of about nine hundred miles. Now and then this coastal voyage was even longer.

This, for a slaver's captain, mates and crew, was the most hated and feared part of the vessel's whole voyage. Disease was a constant threat and ship-owners did not easily forgive a master who lost a large number of his black captives before reaching the Sugar Islands. Also, all had to be constantly alert for signs of a slave revolt. There are records of rebellions aboard some slavers, either along the Guinea Coast or in the Middle Passage, in which every white man aboard the ship was murdered.

And always there was the blasting heat of the tropical sun, the humidity and the stench, which got worse as the *Sukey* moved along the coast. If the hardships endured by the white men aboard a slave ship on the Guinea Coast seem terrible, what of the wretched black men and women in the 'tween decks?

There were sanitary arrangements of sorts aboard the *Sukey*, of course. The captain, mates and crew had their toilet facilities, known to seafaring men as "the head," which were rude but kept reasonably clean in most vessels. The arrangements for the slaves were much different. In the hold were placed three or four wooden tubs, each about two feet wide at the bottom, a foot at the top, and twenty-eight inches high. There were not enough of them and they were not large enough to take care of the needs of the human cargo.

Worst of all, it was almost impossible for most

of the slaves to reach the tubs. A guard had to un-
lock a slave's leg shackle first. Then the miserable
captive had to stumble, bent over because of the
low overhead, across the bodies of the others between him and the tub in the dimness of the 'tween
decks. It was almost impossible to avoid stepping
on someone and this often caused disturbances and
fights.

Many of the captives could not bear such an or-
deal and relieved themselves where they lay. The
floors soon became covered with excrement, often
mixed with blood, for the shackles were apt to
chafe the slaves' legs until they bled when they
tried to change their cramped positions.

Of course, the tubs were emptied each day, and
when the weather was good the slaves could be
brought on deck and the 'tween decks cleaned after
a fashion. Sailors would be sent below with brooms,
swabs and buckets of vinegar heated by dropping
red-hot bullets into them. In this way some sort of
cleanliness was maintained, but it was a poor one
at best, and nothing could take away the fearful
smell. For many a young fellow his first slaving
voyage was his last, especially if he had any pity in
his heart.

As slaves were picked up at one factory after another, their confinement in the hot, humid, foul

'tween decks made them desperate. They were ready to take any chance to get away, even if failure almost certainly meant death. Mutinies and attempts to escape often did happen along the coast, and some succeeded.

Aboard one ship, on the coast of the Bight of Biafra, the slaves managed to free themselves from their shackles and charged up to the main deck. Their guard, the rest of the crew and the mates saw that they could not possibly hold off so many men, and all jumped overboard.

Only the captain remained. The leader of the mutiny, a giant slave, made a rush for him, his hands raised, ready to bring the handcuffs dangling from his wrist down on the skipper's head. But the captain slipped swiftly into the cabin, where the arms and ammunition were kept, lit a fuse and held it sizzling to the bunghole of a powder cask.

The leader of the mutiny retreated to the main deck, shouting that the ship was about to blow up. Then he and the rest of the mutineers jumped overboard. Some who could swim reached shore; the rest drowned or were eaten by sharks.

The sufferings that have been described were not the only ones the slaves endured. Much will be told of their daily life in a later chapter on the horrors of the Middle Passage. It is enough for now only to add that even men confined in the damp, cold, rat- and vermin-infested dungeons of medieval prisons probably suffered no more than these pitiful human beings who had fallen into the hands of greedy, brutal white men.

At last, after five months that seemed to all more like five years, the *Sukey,* with 120 slaves, left the African coast and sailed westward over the Middle Passage for Cuba. But before describing that voyage it will be well to learn something of how slaves were obtained in the interior of West Africa and brought to the forts and factories on the coast.

The harbor of Boston, one of New England's major seaports, about 1835. Painting by Ambroise Louis del Garneray; aquatint by Sigmund Himely

At left, men, women and children are captured during a raid on an African village. Below, the captives are led to the coast to be sold as slaves

*A slaver
at anchor off
the Guinea Coast*

*The lower deck of a slave ship, filled with
its human cargo, shown in a diagram*

Loading a slave ship

An antislavery cartoon of 1833 shows slaves being thrown overboard in mid-Atlantic

Cuban slaves plant sugar cane (above)
and harvest it (below)

On a West Indian plantation, the great house overlooks a windmill-powered sugar mill

Feeding cane into a grinding mill

Soldiers put down a slave revolt in Santo Domingo

On a beach at Antigua, barrels of molasses are loaded for shipment to New England

4.

The Hunters' Country
and Their Prey

LONG BEFORE EUROPEANS FIRST CAME TO WEST
Africa in the fifteenth century, powerful, rich black
empires existed there. The first one of which there
are historical records is Ghana. Before the year
1000, Ghana ruled over most of the northwestern
part of West Africa, south of the great Sahara Desert and southeast to the River Niger.

The king of Ghana ruled over many subjects. He
could put an army of two hundred thousand soldiers into action. And while Ghana did not have
some of the advantages of European civilization—
the wheel, for example, was then unknown in West
Africa—it had its own advanced civilization.

A system of laws kept order in the country. Agri-
cultural skill enabled the people to raise a variety
of crops in plenty. They knew the value of certain
herbs in healing injuries and curing disease. Their

towns had excellent buildings, and connecting these centers was a good system of roads, with rest houses along them where travelers could stop overnight.

More than one great empire has flourished and then faded away for one reason or another. In ancient times the vast and powerful Roman Empire, which for many years controlled a large part of the known world, finally collapsed. In the nineteenth century the British Empire grew to such an extent that it was said the sun never set on British possessions. Yet today it is gone; most of its colonies are completely free and independent, bound to Britain only by membership in the British Commonwealth of Nations. And so it happened with Ghana, as well as with other West African empires.

Ghana was first replaced in the eleventh century by the empire of the Mandingos, called Mali. The Mandingos founded Timbuktu, but were replaced in turn by the Songhai Empire.

In 1590 the Moors of North Africa crossed the Sahara Desert, overthrew the Songhai and captured Timbuktu. Located on the long Niger River, which flows southeastward into the Gulf of Guinea, the city was a natural trading center. Under the Moors it became rich and famous.

The Moors brought with them their culture and

the Mohammedan religion. They founded a university at Timbuktu that became known throughout the world for its faculty of scholars, whose knowledge rivaled that of the foremost scholars of Europe. Moorish missionaries also converted many West African natives to Mohammedanism.

It is not strange that when the former British colony of the Gold Coast gained its independence in 1956, the new republic took the name of Ghana, for it had been a part of the great empire of Ghana in ancient times. Nor is it strange that the French colony of Sudan, once part of the Mandingo Empire of Mali, should have called itself the Republic of Mali when it too became independent in 1960. Both names have a proud heritage.

There were other great kingdoms in West Africa. An important one, for example, was Benin, now part of the Republic of Nigeria. The king of Benin, called the Oba, lived in the capital, also called Benin, in an enormous palace. The city of Benin was surrounded by a wall ten feet high and six miles long. Inside were broad streets and houses made of red clay polished to such a luster that an early explorer who visited Benin thought they were made of red marble.

Yet the magnificence of these rich kingdoms did not last. The Moors, penetrating toward the Guinea

Coast, raided, looted and destroyed many towns. The people also suffered from raids by savage cannibal tribes. But they kept the culture they had developed.

Near the coast were a number of towns as large as some important European cities. West Africans had their own imaginative style of architecture. They could weave cloth into beautiful patterns and colors. They raised great herds of cattle, sheep and goats. They could smelt iron and work it into useful tools and utensils. They worked in brass, too, and were expert sculptors and wood-carvers. Examples of African craftsmanship are among the prized possessions of museums the world over.

Also important was their music, which West African slaves brought with them to the West Indies and the American colonies. Much of our jazz and other forms of modern American music developed from it.

And like other peoples throughout the world, the West Africans had their own folklore—stories and myths that were handed down from one generation to the next by being told and sung.

Early white explorers heard some strange tales. They were told of a place richer in gold than the fabled El Dorado that Spanish conquistadors had sought in vain in the Americas—a region where gold dust was as common as dirt and jewels as common as pebbles. It was said that on the island of Madagascar, off the faraway eastern coast of Africa, lived huge birds called rocs that were so large they could swoop down on elephants and fly away with them. There were stories of pygmies only six inches tall, of people with lower lips so large they could fling them over their heads as protection from the tropical sun and of course of cannibals, including one tribe who used to knock down their victims with their powerful tails before eating them. Naturally, all these things were myths and legends.

Communication among people from different parts of West Africa was difficult, however, for each tribe had its own language and members of one tribe usually could not understand the speech of another. And there were no written languages until, toward the end of the eighteenth century, one of the Mandingo tribes invented a way of writing down its speech.

In the fifteenth century, white men came to the Guinea Coast. The Portuguese were first, followed by the other European nations already mentioned. And soon the slave trade was in full swing.

The most prized slaves came from the Gold Coast. Most of them belonged to the Ashanti kingdom,

about a hundred miles into the interior. But the
Ashantis were among the proudest, most independent and warlike nations of all West Africa. They
fiercely resisted being sold into slavery in the West
Indies. They would risk any punishment, even
death, for attempting to escape; in fact, they would
often hang themselves if they were treated harshly
and could manage to put an end to their sufferings.

Still, even though the Ashantis led some of the
bloody revolts in the West Indies, where they were
called Coromantees, they were considered the best
and most faithful of slaves. A governor of the Leeward Islands (the northern group of the long chain
of small islands running north and south in the Caribbean) wrote in the eighteenth century, "There
was never a raskal or coward of that nation." He
added that "no man deserved a Coromantee that
would not treat him as a friend rather than a slave."

Next most valued among the West African people
were those of the Slave Coast. Most belonged to the
Yoruba or Dahomey tribes and were industrious
people, skilled in cultivating the soil and less apt to
make trouble.

At the southeast end of the Guinea Coast lay the
dreaded Bight of Biafra, also called the Calabar
Coast. Here the shorelands were swampy—breeding
places for malaria and other diseases. But the Bight

of Biafra had one advantage—its chief ports of New Calabar, Bonny and Old Calabar lay on rivers so that slave ships could be sheltered from the murderous surf and the violent tropical storms that often raged along the Guinea Coast.

In this region a large number of the slaves came from the Ibo tribe, with some from the Ibibos and Efiks. It was a popular trading area, although the Ibos loved their homeland so much that when they were sold into slavery in the Sugar Islands they often hanged themselves.

Another large slave trading region was in the north, called by the map makers Senegambia because it lay between the great Senegal and Gambia rivers. There were a number of tribes here, of which the most important were the Foulahs (it is spelled in several ways) and Mandingos. The Foulahs were light colored people, whose chief occupation was raising large herds of cattle. Many were Mohammedans, and some of the young men of the wealthier families had learned to read and write in Arabic, the Mohammedan language. The Mandingos were justly famous; some owned vast plantations like the white planters of the West Indies, and like these white planters they had many slaves.

Senegambia was rich in gold dust, ivory, iron, salt and slaves. Few of the Senegambian slaves made good field workers. Because of their high intelligence and skills they were more apt to be used on the West Indian plantations as house servants or as artisans such as coopers and blacksmiths.

White traders obtained slaves from these areas in various ways. Like all peoples throughout history, these West African tribes had their wars. Captives, unless they were killed, were enslaved by the chiefs or kings of the tribes, and many were sold to black planters. As slaves they had no rights at all. And since West African kings, unless they were devout Mohammedans, followed ancient religious rites that often included human sacrifices, these slaves were sometimes sacrificed, usually by beheading, at religious ceremonies.

But on the whole, the slave of an African owner was treated better than one belonging to a white owner in the West Indies. It was possible for a slave in West Africa to gain his freedom; in the Sugar Islands this usually happened only if slaves were able to escape and not be caught.

Chiefs and kings who had slaves they could spare were willing to barter them when white slave traders came into the interior. And when the demand for slaves became great, the rulers of the interior kingdoms were encouraged to obtain even more slaves by making war on neighboring tribes and taking captives. So tribal wars increased greatly.

More and more often a tribe would make war on a neighboring one with which it had no quarrel.

Black owners of slaves were tempted by the trade goods the white men brought in their caravans— the brightly colored clothes, beads, necklaces and other ornaments—but even more popular were muskets and powder with which they could wage wars and obtain more slaves. Most prized of all, however, was rum, which the white man had introduced into Africa. Artful traders dashed black slave-owners lavishly with rum, while they cunningly weakened their own drinks with water. A slave-owner whose wits were befuddled by strong rum could be cheated more easily.

The traders also used rum to enlist the help of witch doctors. Although some natives were converted to Mohammedanism (which forbids the use of any alcoholic drink), many more were not. And in many African religions, the witch doctor was a mighty man.

A professor of religion at the University of Ghana in West Africa, who was lecturing in the United States, declared that descriptions of witch doctors as wearing terrifying masks, casting spells, driving evil spirits from sick people and performing magic had been invented by foreign writers. He called the witch doctors master herbalists.

Master herbalists they certainly were. They understood the healing properties of many herbs and the leaves and bark of shrubs and trees that were unknown to the doctors of Europe. Yet, with all respect to the learned professor, many witch doctors did not forget that the appearance of magic in their healing impressed people with no medical knowledge. And many of the stories told by early white slave traders show that witch doctors were no different from other men the world over. There were unscrupulous ones who would do anything for profit.

The white slave traders would dash these unscrupulous witch doctors with rum and other trade goods. The witch doctor would then announce that black magic was going on in the town. The entire population would be ordered to assemble in the central square, and the witch doctor would go through the crowd sniffing loudly. He was "smelling out" his victims. Those he pointed out—always strong, healthy men and women—were charged with practicing black magic, dragged out and sold to the white traders.

Sometimes people were kidnaped by their own tribesmen and sold into slavery. When there were famines, tribesmen would seize their neighbors and exchange them for food from the trader's caravan. Occasionally, men sold themselves to keep from starving. But by far the greatest number of slaves were captives taken in wars.

Once a trader had enough slaves, he would fasten them in a line to a long rope, an arrangement called a coffle, and march them to one of the factories or castles on the coast. If all or part of the journey could be made down a river, the slaves would be thrown like so many sacks of meal into the bottoms of boats that were always damp and sometimes leaky and awash with water. In this way the slaves finally arrived at the coast, where they were sold again, loaded into the slave ships and transported over the Middle Passage to the West Indies.

5.

The Terrible
Middle Passage

LITTLE IS KNOWN OF THE *Sukey's* WESTWARD VOYAGE across the Atlantic, but apparently she reached Havana with all or most of her human cargo still alive. Nor do we know how Captain Almy treated his slaves during the voyage. There were humane shipmasters who did all they could to ease the misery of that voyage, and there were bad ones who treated the slaves cruelly and sometimes even murdered them.

Captain Almy may have been one of the latter sort. One writer on the history of the Rhode Island slave trade tells of a rumor in Bristol that the *Sukey's* captain (it may have been someone else since his name and the date of the voyage are not given) had thrown several slaves overboard, probably because they showed symptoms of the dreaded smallpox. The story goes on to say that the doomed black people managed to cling to the taffrail at the stern of the ship, and that the captain chopped their hands off.

The *Sukey*'s owner, Captain Jim deWolf, had at least one shameful stain on his record. In 1791, while Captain Jim was making slaving voyages himself, a Federal grand jury in Rhode Island charged him with murder for throwing a female slave overboard on the Middle Passage when he discovered she had smallpox. But the captain could not be found, and for four years he remained out of sight. When the case against him was dropped, he returned to his evil business and became a rich slaveship owner.

Captains of slavers were known either as "tight packers" or "loose packers," depending upon how many slaves they crammed into the space they had. There were shipowners so greedy that captains, in order to carry as large a slave cargo as possible, had to nest the black people spoon-fashion—lying on top of each other in the hold. Since most New England slave ships were small, because they could be run more profitably than the larger ones the British and some other nations preferred, tight packing was likely to be used in them. In the last half of the eighteenth century most slaver captains were tight packers. Considering the *Sukey*'s length of only seventy feet and her cargo of 120 slaves, she was probably tightly packed.

Because Captain Almy finished loading his slaves at Grand Popo, he doubtless had put provisions and water aboard there before sailing directly to Cuba. Ships trading farther south in the Bight of Benin and Bight of Biafra often had to put in at one of the Portuguese islands lying off those coasts for more supplies, and this caused delay. The quickest time by the shortest route from the Gambia River to the West Indies island of Barbados was about three weeks, but Captain Almy had about 1,200 more miles to sail, well over 4,000 miles in all.

Slavers tried to make the fastest time possible to the West Indies. However, a ship might run into a calm that kept her drifting slowly, often in the wrong direction, for days, or a violent storm could drive her hundreds of miles off her course. The Middle Passage could last as long as three months. At such times everyone aboard was on short rations of food and was allowed as little as a cupful of water a day, which was all the slaves got anyway.

Short or long, the Middle Passage was an endless misery for the slaves. It was bad enough when the weather was good; if it was stormy their life was agony.

In clear weather the slaves were unshackled and

brought up to the main deck, where the men were
shackled again to long chains running along the
bulwarks on each side of the vessel. The women
and children were allowed to roam about as they
pleased.

About nine o'clock in the morning they were
given their first meal. Those from the northern
sweep of the Guinea Coast had boiled rice, millet
or cornmeal. Sometimes a few lumps of meat were
thrown in to help keep the slaves healthy. Slaves
from the Bight of Biafra were fed stewed yams.
Those from still farther south in the River Congo
region preferred the starchy manioc or cassava flour,
or bananalike plantains. And at this time they re-
ceived their daily half-pint of water in a small pan
called a pannikin.

After breakfast the slaves were "danced," in order to give them exercise. Still shackled to the bulwarks, the men had to jump up and down as best
they could until often the flesh of their ankles was
raw and bleeding from the irons around them. Those
who were free of their bonds were better able to
dance to the rhythm that was pounded out on an
African drum or an iron kettle, sometimes to the
accompaniment of music played by a sailor on a
fiddle or African banjo. It is not hard to imagine
how much "pleasure" the miserable black people

had from such dancing. Nor is it strange that when they were made to sing while they danced, the songs were of misery, fear, hunger and homesickness.

During this time members of the crew roved about the deck carrying whips, which were generally just pieces of rope. The wicked cat-o'-nine-tails—nine tarred cords, each with a knot at its end —was seldom used aboard American slavers. The "cat," as it was called, could slash the skin of a slave's back to ribbons in a few lashes.

While the slaves were on deck, some of the sailors were sent below to clean up the sickening mess in the 'tween decks. In some ships the captains saw to it that as good a job as possible was done every day —washing and scrubbing with swabs and brooms, then rinsing with hot vinegar. Others left the cleaning until a week had passed. Some humane captains even had the slaves bathe—in sea water of course— every day.

In the late afternoon came the slaves' second and only other meal. Sometimes it was the same as breakfast, but many slaver captains fed their cargoes horse beans—large beans used to feed horses— because they were the cheapest food. The beans were boiled until they were pulpy and then covered with a mixture of palm oil, flour, water and, to cover up the bad taste, plenty of red pepper. This was called "slabber sauce."

After their meal, the slaves were taken back to the 'tween decks and shackled for the night. Living there was bad enough in good weather, for the place was always stifling. In a storm it was far worse. Then the gratings on each side of the ship were covered with tarpaulins so that great waves, breaking over the main deck at times, could not reach the 'tween decks. This made the heat even greater, and reduced the supply of air. Slaves near the gratings struggled to put their noses to the covered openings for a little of the precious air that filtered through; the rest simply lay there, gasping for breath.

Some went insane. Some suffocated. Those who went mad were sometimes brought on deck and flogged to death, sometimes clubbed over the head and pitched overboard. To end their suffering, some slaves committed suicide by jumping overboard if they saw a chance. Some found ways to cut their throats. Others refused to eat.

Slavers used a vicious instrument called a "speculum oris" to feed slaves who tried to starve themselves. It looked much like a pair of dividers. The legs were closed and the instrument forced into the slave's mouth. Then a thumb screw was turned, opening the legs and forcing the black man's jaws apart so that food could be crammed down his throat.

The moment a telltale scab of smallpox appeared on a slave's face he was instantly thrown overboard so that others might not become infected. Some fell ill of dysentery, caused by the indescribable filth in which they lived, and those usually died.

Even aboard slavers where captains treated their black cargoes well and gave them plenty to eat, slaves sometimes died, apparently just because they wished to live no longer. Perhaps it could truly be said they died of broken hearts.

Most voyages over the Middle Passage were, mercifully, quite fast. The westward course first took the vessel a little to the north, and in the latitude of Cape Verde she would fall in with the trade wind, usually blowing steadily from the northeast. For most of the voyage, if the weather held good, the ship would bowl along, driven by a spanking breeze at her stern.

The danger of mutiny lessened once a slaver was well at sea, since the slaves did not know how to navigate a ship. It became greater again once she approached the Sugar Islands.

The captain of the brig *Sally*, Esek Hopkins, was to become famous in the American Revolution as the first commander-in-chief of the new nation's navy. But on a slaving voyage in 1765 he ran into bad luck.

During the *Sally's* crossing to West Africa part of his cargo of rum leaked out. He managed to load a cargo of slaves on the Guinea Coast, but again ill fortune struck him when most of his crew died of tropical fevers. Short-handed as he was, Captain Hopkins set free some of the slaves in the hold to help work the ship across the ocean. They organized a mutiny. Since Hopkins had arms and the slaves did not, the mutiny was put down, but eighty slaves were killed. And when the *Sally* finally reached the Sugar Islands he had to sell his remaining slaves at a low price, either because there was an oversupply at the time or because his cargo was in poor condition.

There was another danger as a slaver neared the end of the Middle Passage. During the many European and colonial wars between Britain and France in the eighteenth century, the sea teemed with French privateers, ready to seize any British or American ship and her cargo. In the short times of peace between the wars, and after they were ended, these French seizures continued. During the Seven Years' War (called the French and Indian War in the American colonies) from 1756 to 1763, 15 per cent of the slave ships sailing out of Newport, Rhode

Island, were captured by these French marauders. Insurance rates for the vessels (no company would insure the black cargo, anyhow, lest a skipper try to cheat it by throwing his slaves overboard) zoomed up 25 per cent.

But the trade went on. A New England merchant might lose a great deal of money on one voyage and then make it up several times over on the next two or three.

Even after the ships reached the West Indies, the hazards continued. Many foundered on the coral or volcanic reefs of the islands, for in the eighteenth century there were few lighthouses or other beacons to guide vessels safely into harbor.

To make matters worse there were "wreckers" along the island coasts who would set up lights along the shore to make shipmasters think they were approaching a harbor at night. Instead, the vessels were wrecked on razor-sharp reefs and their cargoes stolen.

Legend has it that as late as the nineteenth century one of these land pirates carried on his trade on the coast of Barbados. A rich merchant by the name of Sam Lord, so the story goes, would tie lights to the horns of deer on his plantation to make ship captains think they were approaching the island's capital of Bridgetown. Instead, their ships would be wrecked on Cobbler's Reef, and Sam, a wicked man in other ways as well, would profit by their misfortune. His magnificent great house, Sam Lord's Castle, has been restored and may be visited today.

Ships could also be lost when hurricanes swept the islands, causing terrible havoc. Yet in most cases the dreadful Middle Passage ended safely at last.

The final few days were usually ones of celebration for all, even the slaves. Unless the vessel's provisions and water were almost gone, everyone had plenty to eat and drink. (In the case of the slaves this was done at least partly in order to fatten them up as much as possible for the market.) And all but those slaves who were considered dangerous were released from their confinement.

What lay ahead for the black people from West Africa when they reached the Sugar Islands? Many were terrified of their unknown fate—too often with good cause.

6.

Paradise, Plantations and Punishment

IN THE LAST HALF OF THE EIGHTEENTH CENTURY, when the trade was at its height, most American slavers put in first at one of the British islands of the West Indies because of the higher prices paid for their human cargoes. Barbados was one of the chief slave ports because it lay nearest to West Africa. One of the long chain of small islands—the Lesser Antilles—that runs north and south, it lies about a hundred miles east of the others, on the very edge of the Caribbean Sea, with the Atlantic Ocean lapping at its eastern coast.

There were other markets for slaves, however, for practically all the islands raised sugar cane and needed the black people who could work under the tropical sun. But the larger islands and those that had large areas of land suited to growing sugar cane had the favorite ports. Barbados, not being very mountainous, had immense, fertile fields where the cane grew well.

Another popular British island was Jamaica, even though it lies some twelve hundred miles west of Barbados. It is far larger, being one of the Greater Antilles that run east and west in the northern part of the Caribbean. And although it is mountainous, Jamaica has vast areas of rich soil where sugar cane flourishes. Other smaller, cane-growing British islands, such as Antigua and St. Christopher (also called St. Kitts), also welcomed slavers.

The *Sukey*, however, put in at Cuba, where Captain Jim deWolf owned sugar plantations and grinding mills. She could load molasses cheaply there for the homeward voyage to Bristol.

Whatever the port, the arrival of a slaver caused a great stir and bustle. Usually the town was built near the wharves, around a central square or savanna that was often used as a market by the country people, who brought their vegetables, fruit and handicrafts there to sell. The savanna would be lined with a tavern or two, a few shops and, if the town was the island's capital, as it usually was, government buildings.

There were factors in the Sugar Islands, just as on the Guinea Coast, who bought slaves for plantation owners. Or the owner or his overseer might ride in from the estate somewhere outside the seaport, often a good many miles, to make his own choice. Most owners had no pity for the human beings who became their property; they thought only of the money the slaves would produce for them.

The first slaves to be disposed of were those who were diseased or had been maimed or seriously harmed during the Middle Passage—those whose hands or feet had been lopped off as punishment or those made useless for hard work by savage floggings. All the slaves were brought on deck, and these unfortunate people, who were called "refuse," were picked out and taken ashore to a tavern.

There a vendue or public auction was held "by inch of candle." The auctioneer lighted a candle and bidding for the "refuse" began. When one inch of the candle had burned, the bidding was closed, and these slaves went to the highest bidders. The price was usually about half what a healthy man or woman would bring. Some poor wretches were in such bad shape that no one would buy them, and they were simply turned loose on the wharves. Having no food or water and no means of getting them, they usually died of starvation or thirst.

The healthy slaves were ordinarily sold at a "scramble." The buyers and the captain first agreed upon a price to be paid for each man, woman or child. Then, at a signal, the buyers would rush among the cowering black people, each trying to be the first to seize those he wanted.

The slaves' terror can be imagined. Some thought they were going to be eaten. Occasionally one saw his chance and leaped overboard, but was usually rescued before he drowned.

When the sale was over, the slaves were taken to the estates of their new owners. Often the sugar plantations were at some distance from the seaport, so they had a good chance to see something of the island that was to be their home for the rest of their lives.

The islands of the West Indies are either of coral limestone—the skeletons of untold billions of tiny sea creatures, turned to stone over countless centuries—or of volcanic rock, or both. Some are very mountainous, with high peaks that are often extinct volcanoes. On practically all, the soil is extremely fertile, and anything suited to a tropical climate will grow. The most profitable crop, of course, is sugar cane.

So the slaves, marching under guard to the plantations, might go through rolling country, lush with tropical trees, shrubs and growing crops. They would see not only endless fields of sugar cane, but numerous other trees, fruits and vegetables as well:

coconut palms, fine hardwood trees—including mahogany—bamboo, coffee, cocoa, bananas, citrus
fruits, mangoes, papaws, cassava, nutmeg, cinnamon.
And everywhere were brilliant tropical flowers—red
and purple bougainvillea, red or yellow hibiscus,
scarlet flamboyant, poinsettia and a host of others.

The slaves might gaze in awe at the towering
peaks of mountain ranges. Sometimes the mountain-
tops would be hidden in clouds, marking rain forests, where the rainfall is so great that the peaks are
covered with a thick jungle through which a man
would have to cut his way, and where giant ferns
grow eight or ten feet tall.

If the route lay near the seacoast the slaves might
see miles of shimmering white sand beaches; if the
region were volcanic, the sand might be black. Just
beyond the sand the shallow water would be jade
green, except where curling, white-topped surf
showed that a line of sharp reefs lay just beneath
the surface. Farther out, the color would deepen to
the bright blue of the Caribbean Sea.

This was a paradise, a land of plenty, or rather it
could have been a paradise for the slaves if they
had been free. True, many had been slaves in Africa.
True, there were some among their new masters
who would treat them with great kindness. But too
many of the slave owners, especially in the British,

Spanish and Danish islands, were cruel and brutal.

At last the slaves reached what was to be their new home. Their first view of it would have been the sight of the owner's mansion, or "great house," as it was called, usually on a low hill above the plantation itself. In the second half of the eighteenth century the great houses were impressive and stately. They were built of strong coral limestone blocks or seasoned tropical hardwood, particularly mahogany, or both. Inside, the rooms were large, high-ceilinged for coolness and luxuriously furnished.

Sometimes the road leading down from the hill where the great house stood passed through an arched gateway at the bottom, handsomely carved in scrollwork and painted white. And there, below the hill, were the overseers' houses and office, workshops for blacksmiths, carpenters, masons and coopers, the sugar works and the slaves' houses, laid out in streets.

A slave's house was not too different from an African hut, except for the lower part. There, instead of a sun-baked wall of mud, several wooden posts were driven into the ground. The spaces between them were "wattled" with interwoven twigs and the chinks plastered with clay. The roof was thatched with grass, palm or coconut leaves.

Inside, there were two rooms. One might be used for cooking, or this might be done out of doors, with a rude shed of planks to be used when it rained. The floor of the hut was bare earth, beaten to make it hard. For beds the slaves had a platform of boards, covered with a mat woven of rushes. There might be a rough table, a stool or two, a few earthenware pans called yabbas, an iron pot, and cups, a dipper and pitcher made from a tough-shelled gourd called a calabash.

The harsh clanging of a bell or the raucous blast of a conch shell horn broke the stillness of the dawn —or night if it was the harvest season—and roused the slaves the morning after their arrival on the plantation. Those who did not tumble out of their huts at once felt the sting of the whips carried by those in charge.

They were assembled outside in a group so that the plantation overseer could look them over. From long experience, he could tell a Mandingo tribesman from a Foulah, an Ibo from a Coromantee at a glance. This and other things he saw told him how to divide the slaves among the three forces or gangs that worked the sugar plantation, along with a fourth group whose duties would be quite different.

The overseer was a man of great power, for he was responsible to the estate owner, the master, for the running of the plantation. He must see that the slaves were put to doing what they were best fitted for and did their work properly. The sowing, cultivating, cutting and harvesting of the sugar cane, the operation of the sugar mill—in fact, everything on the plantation itself—was under his supervision, with the aid of his assistants. Often the owner would spend much time in Europe; sometimes he lived there and seldom came to the West Indies estate. In such cases the overseer was like the master himself.

The best overseer was the one who could get the most work out of the slaves, produce the most sugar and molasses of good quality and in that way make the most money for the owner. Some overseers did this without too much harshness to the black people; others believed that hard, cruel driving of the slaves produced the best results.

Now the overseer would point out a man or woman here, others there, to be put into the first or "great gang," as it was called. It did not matter that the slaves could not understand a word of the English, French, Spanish or other language he spoke. His assistants herded together those picked for the "great gang" and marched them off, with those of this gang that had been on the plantation before, to the cane fields or the sugar mill.

The overseer would pick the strongest and healthiest of the slaves for the great gang. Its members dug and planted sugar cane, cleared land of trees and underbrush for new cane fields, did the hard work of cutting the sugar canes when they were ripe, loaded and carted them to the sugar mill and cleared away the refuse of the long, spear-shaped leaves of the cane. Some worked in the mill itself.

These slaves were likely to be Coromantees from the Gold Coast, Dahomans or Yorubas from the Slave Coast, or Ibos from the Bight of Benin, since these people were among the strongest and best field workers. The Coromantees, however, were proud and fierce. It was not easy to train them as slave workers and they had to be watched. With the Mandingos, they were the most likely to plot a revolt or escape.

The second gang was made up of the bigger boys and girls, along with old or infirm slaves. There were not likely to be elderly people among the new arrivals; most of these had lived on the plantation for years. This gang did the weeding in the cane fields and other tasks that did not require great strength.

The third gang was composed of young children, in the charge of an old slave woman. They did all sorts of odd jobs, such as weeding and hoeing the gardens near the slaves' huts that supplied most of their food and collecting feed for the livestock.

The fourth group was separate from the three gangs. It was usually made up of the most intelligent of the slaves, especially those from Angola and the region of the great Congo River, and from Senegambia in the north, including the Mandingos and Foulahs. These were the lucky ones.

Some became domestic servants. In the great houses of large plantations there would be from twenty to forty servants. Each white child had a black nurse, and usually each nurse had an assistant. There were butlers, cooks, grooms to care for the family's horses, and chambermaids. In Martinique each member of an owner's family had at least one personal servant; in wealthy families each white person could have anywhere from three to six attendants.

These black domestics were usually better treated than the field workers and often had a share of the luxurious food of the great house—fresh meat, many kinds of delicious tropical fish, turtle and other delicate seafood.

Also included in this group were intelligent black men who could be trained as artisans—blacksmiths to do horseshoeing and ironwork, coopers to make and repair hogsheads for the molasses, masons for stonework and others. They too were better treated than the field workers.

Laboring in the cane fields was hard, exhausting work. The working day was long—from sunrise or earlier to sunset, and on moonlit nights in harvest time well into the night. Yet these workers had one advantage over the other two regular gangs. They were frequently given salt beef and fish—something the other two did not have—so they would remain strong and healthy.

The work began with the sowing. First, the great gang dug deep trenches. Into them the seed was placed. Cane seeds are buds or eyes that grow along the stem of a cane from four to eight inches apart. In a field in which cane had been cut, eyes below the ground in the stubble that was left would sprout and produce new sugar cane. Several crops could be grown this way, but in time new seeding would be necessary.

Next came cultivation. In that humid, hot climate, weeds grow faster and larger than they do on farms in the United States, so the great gang, aided by the second gang, was kept busy hoeing the ground around the canes to destroy the weeds and loosen the soil.

Before it is ready for harvesting, sugar cane grows eight or ten feet tall, sometimes higher. The only part of the harvested plant that contains the sweet juice is the cane or stem that is anywhere from half an inch to three inches thick. The leaves are of little use except as bedding for the livestock. Even today, on some West Indian sugar plantations, the leaves in a cane field are set afire to destroy them before the canes are cut. However, this often produces a poor grade of sugar or molasses.

Cutting the woodlike canes was no easy job. It took a strong man or woman and a sharp-edged cutting blade, and to do it quickly and efficiently required experience. The slaves used strong, very sharp knives and also billhooks, heavy curved knives that were also very sharp.

There were nuisances and dangers. Cane fields were often infested with cane rats that lived on the cane juice. Traps had to be set for them constantly. And on some of the islands, especially Martinique, the thick cane fields were hiding places for the deadly fer-de-lance, a large snake of the rattlesnake family.

On at least two of the islands, Jamaica and Martinique, the fearless little mongoose, a weasel-like animal, was imported in modern days from Asia to kill both the cane rats and poisonous snakes. It proved so successful in Jamaica that today there are no poisonous snakes and almost no others on the island. But the mongooses, having disposed of the rats and snakes, began killing poultry. Since they are lightning-fast, it is difficult to catch or shoot them, and now they are considered pests in Jamaica.

When the canes were cut they were loaded into carts drawn by horses, mules, oxen or donkeys, and taken to the sugar mill. The grinding mills into which the canes were fed were quite simple. The canes were thrust between two grooved cylinders or rolls, and these were revolved, squeezing out the precious juice. The rolls were turned in three ways. In some cases long wooden arms extended out from the shafts of the rolls. Cattle, oxen, mules or horses were harnessed to the arms and driven around and around to make the rolls revolve. In other cases, the power was furnished by a great windmill. And in mountainous country, where a stream tumbled down a steep hillside, a gigantic water wheel would do the work.

The juice squeezed from the canes was purified by adding lime and then boiled in big stone pots, turning into thick, sweet molasses. Some was crystallized into the sugar used at that time; it was not filtered or bleached to make it white as it is today, but was brown loaf sugar, generally called muscavado. The crushed cane stalks, called bagasse, were used as fuel for boiling the cane juice.

The Sugar Islands had their own distilleries to make rum from molasses but, unlike today when

West Indies rum is considered the finest in the world, New England rum was then by far the best in quality, and most of the molasses went into big hogsheads to be shipped north. New England distilleries were demanding more and more molasses so that the rum distilled from it could be exchanged for more and more slaves on the Guinea Coast.

Some slaves in the West Indies worked willingly enough. They were accustomed to a hot climate. They had plenty to eat, for they raised vegetables and tropical fruit of all kinds in their own gardens. Since they were usually able to raise more food than they needed, some plantation owners allowed them to sell the excess, as well as baskets, utensils, wood carvings and other things they made. Their masters gave them a small supply of working clothes each year, but often with the money they made they would buy bright-colored materials and ornaments to wear on Sundays and on such big holidays as Christmas and Easter.

If this had been all there was to life as a slave in the Sugar Islands, the blacks might have been happy enough, but for two things: they were slaves, and on most plantations they were punished severely for small offenses and with terrible ferocity for higher crimes.

On most of the islands, punishment for any form

of rebellion was unbelievably brutal and inhuman. The Virgin Islands, today largely a territory of the United States, were under Danish control in 1733, and in that year the Danish Royal Council issued an announcement concerning punishment of slaves.

The leader of runaway slaves was to be pinched three times with red-hot iron tongs and then hanged. Other runaways were each to lose one leg unless their owners pardoned them; in that case one ear was to be cut off and each was to receive 150 stripes, or lashes, with the whip. Any slave who knew of others' plans to run away and did not tell his master was to be branded on the forehead and receive a hundred stripes. On the other hand, a slave who turned informer against his fellow blacks planning an escape was to get ten Danish rix-dollars for each slave in the plot.

Regardless of whether his master was willing to pardon him, if a runaway slave was gone twelve weeks or more, one leg was to be chopped off. If he stayed away six months his sentence was death unless his owner pardoned him; then he only lost a leg.

A slave who tried to poison his master would be pinched three times with red-hot tongs and then broken on the wheel, which meant he would be stretched across a wheel and tied to it while all his bones were broken by a man with an iron crowbar. A slave who threatened and struck a white person was pinched and hanged if the white person demanded it; otherwise his right hand was chopped off.

There were many other penalties and restrictions —against carrying weapons of any kind, being in town after drumbeat at sunset, failing to step aside and let a white person pass, holding dances or feasts or beating drums without the master's permission. When a slave was accused of a crime, one white witness was enough to convict him. And a slave even suspected of a crime could be "tried" by torturing him to make him confess.

It was no better on most of the islands. In Jamaica a number of small offenses could be punished by death or by cutting off an arm or leg or by flogging. Even for carelessness or neglect in carrying out some task or order, a slave could be whipped with a switch made of tough lancewood while he hung by his hands. Sometimes the lash of the whip was made of tough fibers of a certain plant, twisted up and knotted until it was almost as hard as iron and would cut like a razor. In some cases, after a whipping, salt and pepper were rubbed into the bloody welts on a slave's back. For a small crime, a slave could be punished by having thrust into his mouth one of the spurs used by horsemen, with its metal wheel or rowel studded with sharp points. Or the slave might have half his foot cut off.

Jamaican slaves who rebelled or those who struck a white man twice were condemned to be burned. A man who visited Jamaica in the early part of the eighteenth century wrote of seeing such an execution: ". . . he is carried to the Place of Execution, chained flat on his Belly, his Arms and Legs extended, the Fire is set to his feet, and so he is gradually burnt up." The same man said other slaves committing crimes were starved to death with a loaf of bread hanging, out of reach, in front of them.

In the French West Indies, under the *Code Noir* (Black Law) of 1685, equally horrible punishments could be given, but masters could not take the law into their own hands as they did on other islands. An accused slave must be tried before a magistrate, where he at least had a chance to defend himself. Nor could an owner torture a slave to make him confess. And a master might free a slave if he wished to do so. This did happen quite often, and if a freed slave married a black woman, she too was free. The only punishment a plantation owner could deal out himself was a light whipping.

The *Code Noir* seems to have been pretty well obeyed, and it was claimed that plantation owners on Martinique and other French islands got more work out of their slaves and were able to run their plantations more efficiently and at a higher profit. Perhaps that is why they could sell molasses to the New England slavers in the Triangular Trade, when slave-ship captains would sell their slaves on a British island at a higher price but buy molasses more cheaply in a French port.

7.

How the Slaves Struck Back

WATCHMEN KEPT STRICT GUARD AT ALL TIMES OVER the slaves on the plantations, especially over those from the strongest, fiercest and most freedom-loving tribes. Yet there were plenty of escapes. In most cases, searching parties captured the runaways, or traitors betrayed them. But on many of the islands, particularly the large and the mountainous ones, a runaway who could reach the dense jungle of the interior or the deep valleys hidden in the clefts of the mountains could gain his freedom and live in hiding.

Sometimes it might be a lone man; in other cases it was a group of slaves who planned carefully, waited their chance and got away. In a group of islands such as the Virgins, some islets would be uninhabited. If runaways could obtain a boat and reach one of these small islands they might live there in safety.

The most famous of all slave escapes took place in 1655. The Spaniards, first to introduce black slavery into the West Indies, had brought many slaves to Jamaica. But in 1655 the British invaded the island and drove the Spaniards out.

There are two stories about how what is known as the escape of the Maroons took place. Some say that the Spaniards deliberately turned their slaves loose, hoping they might drive the British out. But many Jamaicans insist that the slaves themselves escaped. At any rate, in 1655 some 1,500 black slaves fled into the mountainous interior of eastern and northern Jamaica.

The escaped slaves were called Maroons, probably from the Spanish word *cimarron,* meaning wild or unruly. And wild they were. They had suffered much at the hands of cruel Spanish masters and they wanted no more of it from the English.

They established settlements in regions so impenetrable that searching parties of Englishmen could not find them. There they grew plantains, grain and yams. For meat they killed wild pigs, and there was plenty of tropical fruit. Meanwhile, under their chief, Juan de Bolas, who was black though his name was Spanish, they made life miserable for the English plantation owners, hoping the conquerors would give up and go elsewhere.

In the night, without warning, they would swoop

down from the hills on a plantation, set fire to the crops in the fields, steal livestock and disappear as quickly as they had come. The English planters had bought their own slaves to work the cane fields and mills, and the Maroons enticed many of them to run away and join them in the mountains.

After eight years of this harassment, the planters were discouraged and at their wits' end. In 1663 they sent Bolas an offer of freedom and land for all Maroons if they would give up their raids. Bolas and a party of his supporters accepted. But the rest of the Maroons scorned the offer and the raids continued. Many owners in the north abandoned their plantations in despair.

The English continued to try to exterminate the remaining Maroons. But their searching parties failed. So did a pack of ferocious dogs sent to hunt the Maroons down. Some five hundred blacks remained free in the remote valleys and jungles of the interior.

More ill fortune struck the English in 1690. The slaves in the Clarendon district of central Jamaica were chiefly the warlike, powerful Coromantees. One of them, Cudjo (the slaves often named their male children after the days of the week on which they were born, and Cudjo means Monday), organized an escape that succeeded. Many slaves from the Clarendon plantations fled to the safety of the mountain forests and valleys.

Under Cudjo's leadership, the runaways joined forces with the Maroons. Together they established well-hidden settlements, those in the western part of the island under Cudjo's brothers, Accompong and Johnny, and in the east under two subchiefs, Quao (Thursday) and Cuffee (Friday). They had arms, were expert shots and began a serious guerilla war against the English.

Expeditions sent after them were completely baffled. The Maroons could not be induced to fight in the open. Disguised from head to foot in leaves, they set up ambushes and lay in wait for the English. After driving their white enemies back and killing some, the blacks would vanish into the jungle.

The Maroons' settlements were well hidden in the deep clefts between the mountains, and sharp-eyed lookouts would sound an alarm on an abong, a kind of bugle made from a cow's horn, if an English force entered one of the valleys. Maroons from neighboring settlements would then come to help drive the white men off.

This strange war went on for years. In 1734 the English scored a success when a force discovered the Maroon village of Nanny Town (still there today) in the Blue Mountains of eastern Jamaica. Armed with those powerful small cannon called swivel guns, they killed many Maroons and the rest fled. The expedition pursued them and captured some, but the others threw themselves over a precipice rather than return to slavery and the fearful punishments that would await them.

The Maroons were far from beaten, however. A few years later another English expedition was trapped, unable to move ahead or retreat when a forty-eight-hour tropical rainstorm turned streams to raging, impassable torrents. They were attacked by the Maroons, who killed about twenty before the English could make their way back to civilization.

At last a Colonel Guthrie, knowing these blacks could never be exterminated by such forces as the English could raise, proposed that the Maroons be offered complete freedom, land and posts in the government. They were to become a sort of mountain police to be rewarded for returning runaway slaves.

Colonel Guthrie's idea was approved and sent to Cudjo. At first the Maroon leader was suspicious, but he finally agreed to meet Guthrie, though he posted men ready to spring from their hiding places at the first indication of treachery.

No doubt Colonel Guthrie, when he arrived at the meeting place, expected to find a tall, power-

ful, distinguished looking leader. Instead, a hunch-
back with a great lump of flesh on his back came
forward to meet him. Cudjo, who must by that time
have been in his sixties, was short and squat, with
a wild, fierce look. He wore a tattered blue coat,
white knee breeches and a small, round hat. He
carried a musket, wore a powder horn and bag of
shot, and also carried one of the wicked looking
knives the Spaniards used to cut cane, called a
machete.

Each man took off his hat and exchanged it with
the other as a sign of friendship. Then, under a big
tree, they signed the peace treaty. Besides their full
freedom and 1,500 acres of land in northeastern
Jamaica, the Maroons were to receive three pounds
apiece for each runaway slave killed or captured.
And a little later other Maroon settlements were
granted in north-central and northwestern Jamaica.

It may seem that Cudjo and his followers betrayed their own people in agreeing to this arrangement, but it must be remembered that their tribes
in Africa—chiefly Coromantees, Mandingos and Ibos
—had often been enslaved by other tribes and had
enslaved their enemies in return. They seem to have
had no scruples about becoming police for the English and killing runaways or capturing and returning
them.

The Maroons, in their isolated settlements, remained free, wild and fierce. Today they still live in the interior districts of Jamaica and still keep pretty much to themselves.

This was the only mass escape of slaves in the West Indies that succeeded. Nevertheless, there were successful escapes on a smaller scale, and also a number of rebellions. All the rebellions were crushed in time, but the largest, bloodiest and longest was on the island of St. John, in the Virgin Islands.

St. John and neighboring St. Thomas are small islands, but on both there were a great many slaves, most of them from one of the fiercest and most warlike tribes of West Africa, the Aminas of the Gold Coast. By 1733 disorders and escapes had become so frequent that the Danish Royal Council issued its order listing punishments that have already been described. This order touched off the great revolt on St. John.

The slaves appear to have had several leaders, who made their plans with great care and secrecy over a good many months. The punishment order was issued in January, 1733; the revolt broke out in November of that year.

The plotters, supported by many other slaves, waited until Governor Philip Guardelin of the Virgin Islands made a visit to St. John from his capital on St. Thomas. The governor had planned to return to St. Thomas on the day the revolt began, November 13, 1733. The rebellious slaves knew of this and timed the uprising so they could murder him and all the white inhabitants of St. John and then keep the island in their possession as free men.

Some guardian angel must have been watching over Governor Guardelin, as well as over his daughter and her baby, who had come along on the visit. On Saturday morning, November 12, the governor saw a large ship passing just off the coast, heading in the general direction of St. Thomas, and since she appeared to belong to the Danish West India Company, he decided to go back to St. Thomas aboard her. With his daughter and his grandchild he was rowed out in a small boat and taken aboard the ship. They reached St. Thomas safely.

There was a fort on St. John, but it was old, in bad condition and manned only by a sergeant and eight soldiers under the command of a lieutenant. Only two cannon were mounted on its walls.

On Sunday morning, November 13, 1733, a file of slaves carrying bundles of firewood approached the fort. Since this was a common occurrence they were admitted without question. Once inside, the leader gave a signal and the slaves opened their bundles, pulling out knives and cutlasses that had been concealed in the wood. Then they rushed at the soldiers and butchered all but one, who hid under a bed. The lieutenant was not in the fort, but the sergeant was. He leaped through a window in the walls, but in falling to the ground outside injured himself, and the slaves fell upon and murdered him too.

The slaves now had possession of the fort and the twenty-five muskets that were its stock of small arms. The first stage of the plot was accomplished. The fort's captors promptly loaded and fired the two cannon.

This was the signal rebellious slaves all over the island had been waiting for. In mobs they rushed for the great houses.

Some of the planters, hearing the cannon fire, knew what it must mean. With their families they ran to the estate of a Mr. Durlo, whose great house stood on a hill and had cannon mounted to protect it. Those who reached the house were safe for the time being.

Other plantation owners were not so lucky. Rebellious slaves had swarmed into their mansions, killing without mercy. They beheaded a hated judge named Soctman and placed his head on a pole. They also killed his older daughter, but spared her baby sister.

The Durlo estate was on the coast and had a boat. It was sent with all speed to nearby St. Thomas to summon aid, but it seemed that help would come too late to save those in the great house. One brave old Englishman was experienced in handling cannon. Assisted by others, he hurled cannon balls into the mob, killing and wounding many, and the rest retreated down the hill.

Meanwhile, boats arrived from St. Thomas and Tortola, another island in the Virgins. With the cannon to protect them, the planters' wives and children reached the shore and boarded the boats.

Thirty soldiers from the garrison of the fort on St. Thomas and a group of armed citizens of that island landed and stormed the St. John fort, driving the slaves out. Then they headed for the Durlo plantation, where the planters were still holding out against the blacks, who were armed with muskets from the fort and knives fastened to long poles. The force from St. Thomas finally drove them off and rescued the planters.

But everywhere else on the island the story was different. Enraged and bloodthirsty rebels killed everyone they could find except for one man, Dr. Cornelius Bodger, who was spared when he promised to treat the wounded slaves.

Since the force from St. Thomas was too small to overcome the rebels, it returned there with the rescued planters, leaving the slaves in full possession of St. John.

A large vessel from the island of Nevis, manned by sixty men, was engaged by the Danish Royal Council to invade the island, but the attempt failed.

Then the French governor of Martinique sent a strong detachment of four hundred soldiers and officers. Joined by every available man on St. Thomas and the rescued planters of St. John, this formidable force invaded the captured island. Groups landed on both the north and south sides of St. John and fanned out in different directions, driving the rebels ahead of them. The slaves were finally surrounded on the northeast side of the island.

That was the end. The leaders of the revolt held a conference to decide what to do. To surrender was unthinkable. They knew it would mean savage torture, followed by death, either by burning or hanging. Quick death was better.

After holding a feast, they killed themselves. The white invading force first found seven men who appeared to be the leaders. They lay in a ravine, with six guns smashed to pieces by their sides. The seventh musket was undamaged, showing it belonged to the last man to die. A few days later the white force made an even more gruesome discovery —three hundred rebels, all lying dead. There is a legend that these three hundred black men threw themselves over a precipice. It is more likely that they shot themselves and each other.

A few slaves were captured alive. Two were executed on St. John and twenty-six on St. Thomas.

All this did not take place in a day, a week or a month. The slaves had held St. John for six months. During that time they had destroyed forty-four estates, including one owned by the governor, though for some reason they had left forty-eight unharmed.

It was more than a quarter of a century before the slaves of the Virgin Islands tried again to gain freedom. This time the revolt took place on St. Croix, but it failed because one boastful slave in the plot did not know enough to keep his mouth shut.

His name, like that of the Maroon leader, was Cudjo, and he was a slave on Sören Bagge's plantation. One day in December, 1759, he had spoken of Mr. Bagge's great house, saying, "Maybe that house will be mine in a short time." One of his black companions was alarmed. He cursed Cudjo, adding, "You cannot keep a secret." But on the same day Cudjo asked Benjamin Bear, one of the white men on the plantation, how long it would be till Christmas.

"Why do you want to know?" asked Mr. Bear.

"I am asking about it, as I hope by that time to be a *petit-maître*," replied the loose-tongued slave. The French words mean "little master," and are an expression for a dude or dandy.

Mr. Bear seems to have been a trusting soul, for he evidently thought Cudjo was making an idle boast. But the next day, while Bear and another white man were molding bullets on the Bagge plantation, Cudjo asked Bear to give him a dozen of the bullets.

Since Cudjo could not give a reasonable explanation of why he wanted the bullets, Bear refused, but his companion, of an even more trustful nature, gave Cudjo some bullets when Bear was not looking. Nevertheless, Bear heard of it, went to Cudjo and told him sternly that he had better look out or he would find his head lying at his feet.

"You look out that some of your heads won't lie at your feet pretty soon," was Cudjo's insolent reply to Bear and another white man who was with him.

Bear's companion said, "Whom will you then kill?"

"You shall be the first I will kill," replied Cudjo.

By this time Bear was suspicious and alarmed. He reported all he had learned, and the governor ordered Cudjo arrested. In the investigation that followed, Cudjo denied everything. But his brother Quamin (Saturday), who had been brought in and feared some frightful torture, revealed a plot for an uprising and named a number of other slaves who were in it. They were all arrested.

Following a trial, fourteen slaves were sentenced

to death. The apparent chief leader of the plot, a black man who had been given his freedom, committed suicide but the sentence was carried out anyway. A horse dragged his body through the streets by one leg; he was then hanged and burned at the stake.

The punishment of the thirteen living condemned men was just as horrible. Two were broken on the wheel, one living for twenty hours before he died, the other two hours. Two were burned alive. Several were strangled and others hanged.

Ten of the plotters who had played a smaller part were sold into slavery on other islands. Six managed to escape before they could be arrested. A reward of fifty rix-dollars was offered for any of the six captured alive, twenty-five if the man was dead. But of eighty-nine who were suspected, fifty-nine were acquitted because there was not enough evidence against them.

There were other revolts on other islands, but all were quickly crushed. The threat of a murderous uprising haunted plantation owners always, yet one cannot feel too much sympathy toward them. It was greed that made them keep slaves in the first place. Those who lost their lives in the revolts had only themselves to blame, especially the ones who treated their black people harshly. And what human being, enslaved, could live under such systems of punishment as were common in the Sugar Islands without seizing a good chance for freedom and the right to live in peace?

Meanwhile, the Triangular Trade continued to flourish and gold clinked merrily into the coffers of New England merchants and shipowners in their countinghouses. Not that they were the only guilty ones. On the whole, the British, the Spanish and slavers of some other nations were more brutal than American slave-ship captains. Yet the hands of American merchants, shipowners and shipmasters in the slave trade were bloody enough.

8.

Rolling in Money

"THE KING WAS IN HIS COUNTINGHOUSE COUNTING OUT his money," runs the old nursery rhyme. In New England seaports, especially those of Newport, Bristol and Providence in Rhode Island, and Boston and Salem in Massachusetts, it was the merchant-ship owners engaged in the slave trade who spent much time counting their money.

A good deal has already been told of Captain Jim deWolf of Bristol. He was one of five brothers, all of whom took part in slaving at one time or another. He was the richest of the five, though not the greediest. That dubious honor belonged to the oldest, Charles.

There is a story that Charles deWolf invited the Reverend Mr. Henry Wight, minister of the Bristol Congregational Church, to his countinghouse. Mr. Wight saw that there was a pile of stout cloth bags on the floor.

"Parson," said Charles, "I've always wanted to roll in gold." And he threw himself on the heap of money bags and wallowed in them.

The story does not tell what the minister did or said. It would have taken courage to give Charles deWolf a stern lecture on the sinfulness that had brought him all this wealth. His generous contributions no doubt greatly helped to support the Bristol Congregational Church and to pay Mr. Wight's salary. Quite likely, Charles had summoned the pastor there to give him a substantial donation from those money bags, but in doing so he wanted to show off his wealth. Besides, in those days the slave trade was considered perfectly respectable.

A walk through the commercial district of any of the five principal New England slave trading seaports in the latter part of the eighteenth century would have revealed much about the prosperity trade had brought to the town.

Newport is a good example. Like the other ports, the town was centered around the wharves. Thames Street ran past the waterfront, humming with activity. Pudgy merchant-ship owners puffed along between the wharves and warehouses and their countinghouses, perhaps stopping to pass the time of day and talk of trade with each other.

These well-to-do merchants dressed in fine broadcloth coats and knee breeches of rich colors. Brightly embroidered waistcoats bulged over paunches well upholstered by good living. There was lace or ruffles at their necks and the large cuffs of their coats, and they wore white silk stockings and silver-buckled shoes. They were stout, rich, comfortable-looking men, and with good reason.

Along Thames and nearby streets, the merchants' warehouses were chockablock with goods, some brought in by Newport's big fleet of merchant ships, others to be shipped out. Wharves lined the whole waterfront, but sea captains could not always find one vacant and often would have to anchor in the harbor and wait their turn.

In one three-month period, three thousand hogsheads of molasses came into Newport. Three thousand, that is, on which the British tax on molasses had been paid. No one knows how many more were smuggled past the customs officials, but Rhode Islanders were as expert smugglers as they were seafaring men.

All this activity brought prosperity not only to the merchant-ship owners, but also to hundreds of other people. Sandwiched in between the warehouses were sail lofts, where the canvas for Newport ships was repaired and new sails made, and ship chandlers' shops with their many provisions and fittings for vessels. And in 1761 there were at least five ropewalks where strands of tough flax fibers were twisted into cordage.

Prosperity also created a demand for skilled craftsmen. Joiners and cabinetmakers were busy producing furniture and fittings for the splendid houses of the rich. There were silversmiths making beautiful silver punchbowls, cups and other table-ware—and anyone who has seen the workmanship of one of these colonial silversmiths, Paul Revere of Boston, knows what exquisite objects these masters of the art turned out. Paul Revere would be distinguished today for his craftsmanship even if he had never made his famous ride.

The artisans, like the merchants, were easily recognized. They usually had the sleeves of their coats rolled up, wore green cotton waistcoats fastened with red tape, knee breeches, woolen stockings, heavy leather shoes, linen handkerchiefs tied at their necks and the one unmistakable badge of an artisan—a leather apron.

Of course, not all of this activity was due to the slave trade. More than three hundred small coasting vessels traded between Newport and other American ports on the Atlantic coast or engaged in fishing. Many larger ships were in the whaling trade.

One of Rhode Island's richest merchants was

Aaron Lopez, one of the Jewish settlers who had sought refuge from persecution there. From the days of its founder, Roger Williams, Rhode Island had welcomed people of all religious faiths, and in Newport the Jews had built the first synagogue in America. Aaron Lopez was highly respected and honored for his gifts to worthy causes, but he did engage in a few slave trading ventures. However, his great interest was in whaling, and he is said to have had eighty vessels in this trade. Most of his riches came from the manufacture of spermaceti candles from the oil obtained from the sperm whale.

Yet many a Rhode Island merchant made his money in the Triangular Trade. In 1761 Newport had twenty-two distilleries turning out rum at top speed, as well as three sugar refineries. Other New England ports had as many distilleries or more. While rum was the favorite alcoholic drink of New Englanders, they could never have consumed more than a fraction of the Kill-Devil all the distilleries produced. Much of it must have been sold or traded elsewhere. And it is known that in this colonial period, between forty and fifty ships from Newport alone were slavers.

In spite of some voyages that failed, the profits from the slave trade were enormous. On a single voyage in the Triangular Trade, two Newport merchant partners, William Johnston and Peter Brown, made a profit of over 1,300 pounds after all expenses had been paid. This, at the value of the British pound then, equaled over $6,000. In terms of today's money this is not a large sum, but in colonial days it was a small fortune.

In Bristol, by the early part of the nineteenth century, there could be no doubt that Captain Jim deWolf had made plenty of money in the slave trade. One had only to look at his magnificent country home, built in 1808 on an elevation overlooking Bristol and Narragansett Bay.

The Mount, as he called it, was a showplace. Its doors were of solid mahogany from Santo Domingo in the West Indies. Inside, an impressive spiral staircase wound its way from the ground floor to a glass cupola in the roof. The walls of the spacious rooms were frescoed with watercolor scenes by an Italian painter. The mantels over the fireplaces were of Italian marble. The table in the great dining room was set with silverware made by expert craftsmen and Lowestoft china imported from England. There was a huge kitchen, and outside were gardens, stables and a deer park like those on the country estates of English lords. A broad avenue leading to the house was lined with royal palms. All this from the toil, sweat—and blood—of enslaved blacks.

Godfrey and John Malone were among the great Newport merchant-ship owners of the period from 1730 to 1740. Of the two, Godfrey is the more interesting. He did some privateering, some smuggling, and traded to Africa for slaves.

He built a magnificent mansion a mile north of Newport. It was a two-story stone house, luxuriously furnished, and, like Captain Jim deWolf's residence, had a circular stairway leading to a cupola with a view of the town and the sparkling blue waters of Narragansett Bay. Its grounds included a six-hundred-acre farm and a beautifully laid out garden with winding walks, flowers, shrubbery and artificial lakes in which goldfish swam.

Godfrey Malone was fond of the crews who manned his ships. They were rough seafaring men and so was he at heart, in spite of his money, splendid house and fine clothes. So when a ship returned from a successful voyage, the story goes, all hands aboard her would be invited to dinner at the mansion.

On these occasions, Godfrey did not have the table set with its usual fine china. He used cheap, common crockery. But he spared no expense to make the dinner lavish.

When all had eaten, drunk and were merry, Godfrey would rise from his place at one end of the table and hurl a plate at the man opposite him. This was the signal for all to take part, and when the crash and splintering of plates, cups, bowls, tureens and other dishes died down not a single dish would remain unbroken. So did the jolly Godfrey Malone reward his sailormen.

Among the most famous Rhode Island slave traders were the Brown brothers of Providence. Their names were John, Joseph, Nicholas and Moses, but jealous rivals who had not prospered as greatly called them "John and Josey, Nick and Mosey."

They followed their father, Captain James Brown, in the slave trade. He fitted out the first vessel, the sloop *Mary,* to sail from Providence as a "Guinea Man," as slave ships were sometimes called. When she reached the Guinea Coast there were nineteen slavers in the trading area, an oversupply of rum and a shortage of slaves. The *Mary's* captain got his slaves after many weeks, but they were evidently not of high enough quality to bring a good price in the West Indies, and the voyage was no great success.

Captain Brown tried one more slaving voyage, but the ship vanished. Since this was during the time of the colonial wars, she was probably seized by an enemy privateer. And before the wars ended in 1763 the elder Brown died, and his sons took over the business.

The story of the Brown brothers' slave venture with the brig *Sally*, under command of Captain Esek Hopkins, has already been told. That disastrous voyage was enough of the slave trade for all the brothers except John. In 1733 the youngest of them, Moses, became a Quaker and spent the rest of his life trying to get slaving abolished. Evidently what he had seen on slaving voyages he had made so sickened him that he decided there must be no more of it.

Joseph and Nicholas too seem to have had some sober thoughts about the frightfulness of what they were doing. They too left the trade, but they became rich in other kinds of business. With Aaron Lopez they took part in manufacturing spermaceti candles and also owned distilleries, an iron-smelting furnace and a glass-making mill. But John Brown remained in the slave trade until he died after the close of the American Revolution.

There were some skinflints in the slave trade. Probably the worst was Captain Simeon Potter of Bristol. He did not become the richest of the Rhode Island merchants, but he had his finger in a good many pies. He started as a seafaring man, became a captain, then turned privateer, and finally returned to the land, where he dealt in real estate and got into the slave trade, though he never made a slaving voyage himself.

One day one of his nephews who had been un-successful in business came to him and asked him how he could make some money. "Make money! Make money!" growled Captain Potter. "*I* would plow the ocean into pea-porridge to make money!"

And indeed he would do almost anything to make money. In 1764 he sent the sloop *King George* out on a slaving voyage. He wrote instructions to her master, Captain William Earle, as follows:

"Make yr. Cheaf Trade with the Blacks and Little or none with the white people if possible to be avoided. Worter yr. rum as much as possible and sell as much by the short mesuer as you can."

In other words, Captain Earle was to deal with black traders direct if he could, rather than with white factors, because it was easier to cheat the blacks. And he was to cheat the slave traders by weakening the rum with water. By "short mesuer" (measure) Potter meant the captain was to try and cheat the traders by not giving them full gallons of rum if he could get away with it.

Another trick was used by at least one merchant. He had one of his captains buy slaves instead of exchanging rum for them, using counterfeit coins made of pewter instead of silver.

The deWolf brothers were fitting successors to Captain Potter. An old lady who did sewing for the deWolf family described the boys: "They was handsome, dashing and reckless, but for morals something fierce."

Mark Anthony deWolf, their father, was a clerk in Simeon Potter's countinghouse when he married the old rogue's daughter Abigail. He became a sea captain, and a hard one, and he had fifteen children. Most of the boys became either owners or captains of sailing ships.

Five of them entered the slave trade. The story of how Charles, the oldest, rolled in gold has already been told. But his brother, Captain Jim, who owned the *Sukey*, became the richest.

At fifteen he went to sea aboard a privateer, one of the many raiders that sailed the seas during the colonial wars and were little better than pirates. The vessel was captured, and Jim deWolf served some time in prison. By the time he was twenty he was an officer aboard one of the Brown brothers' slavers, and at twenty-six he owned his own brig, the *Little Watt*. He married a wealthy woman, went into the slave trade and became one of the richest men in Rhode Island.

Another of the five brothers, William, did not have the dark, tough look of Jim and Charles. He was a chubby man with a pleasant smile, but it evidently was not the sign of a soft heart, for he owned a dozen slave ships before he retired from the slave trade to head a company that insured vessels against shipwreck, piracy and trouble with Rhode Island's laws against slavery that had been passed in 1787.

The other two boys who took part in the slave trade—Levi, the youngest, and John—soon got out of it. Levi made only one voyage to the Guinea Coast. He came back so revolted by what he had seen that he quit the sea and retired to a little farm, where he read his Bible and prayed each day, probably for forgiveness for that one voyage in the Triangular Trade.

John made several slaving voyages that turned out profitably, but then "swallowed the anchor," the sailor's expression for leaving the sea, and became one of the best farmers in Rhode Island.

No one should think, from all this, that Rhode Island was the only culprit in the slave trade, though at times the colony probably had more slavers than any other. But for her size Rhode Island, with her seafaring tradition, was the leader, and after the Revolution, when the United States government prohibited the slave trade, she kept on with it in an important way for a long time. Nevertheless, the other New England colonies also profited from slaving.

Not as much is known about Massachusetts,

Connecticut and New Hampshire, although all appear to have had some part in the Triangular Trade. But in the case of Massachusetts, the telltale is the distilleries. In 1763 there were sixty-three of them in and around the two main seaports, Boston and Salem, making rum with all possible speed. They turned 15,000 hogsheads of molasses into about 12,500 hogsheads of rum each year. In Boston, the area back of the wharves along Essex Street was crowded with distilleries, and there were others in various parts of the town.

Even this great flood of O-Be-Joyful was not enough to supply the demand. In 1752 a Massachusetts slaver captain was unable to get a cargo of rum for the Guinea Coast. So he decided to try Rhode Island, but the owner's agent there wrote: "We are sorry to find that you are ordering your ship here in expectation of having her loaded with rum in about five weeks. We cannot give you encouragement of getting that quantity of rum these three months, for there are so many vessels loading for Guinea, we can't get one hogshead for cash."

There are scattered records about the slave trade carried on by Boston and Salem merchants in Massachusetts, yet they tell little of how large it was, of the voyages the slave ships made or the profits they brought the merchant-ship owners. But it appears that during the first half of the eighteenth century, Massachusetts was the leader. After that it was Rhode Island.

There is one story of a famous Boston merchant who had a share in a slaving voyage, though if he had lived to know its results he would probably never again have invested another penny of his large fortune in such a venture. He was Peter Faneuil. Today, Faneuil Hall, which he built at his own expense and presented to Boston as a marketplace, still stands in Boston's Dock Square and is known as the "Cradle of Liberty" because the fiery patriot James Otis dedicated it to the cause of liberty in 1763.

Peter Faneuil was one of Boston's best known, richest and most respected citizens. He owned a fine mansion and wore the finest and most costly clothes. People gaped in wonderment at the magnificence of his coach as his splendid horses pranced through the streets. But he was a merchant to the core, and rich as he was he lost no chance to improve his already large fortune. In 1742 he put up half the money to buy and fit out a ship for the Guinea trade. John Catlin, who was to command the vessel, had a quarter share and John Jones, a merchant, the other quarter.

Appropriately, the ship was named the *Jolly*

Bachelor. Peter Faneuil had inherited from his uncle, Andrew Faneuil, a large fortune on the condition that he would never marry, and he never did. But the "jolly" part of the slaver's name certainly did not describe her voyage.

The *Jolly Bachelor* reached Sierra Leone on the Guinea Coast and took on a cargo of seventy-five slaves. But black natives who lived on a group of islands offshore attacked the ship and murdered Captain Catlin and two of his sailors, freed the slaves who were aboard, stripped the *Jolly Bachelor* of her rigging and left.

A white factor at a trading post there, George Burchall, took possession of the stricken ship. He bought provisions, hired a few more sailors and obtained spare sails and rigging from several English slavers there. He appointed a Captain Winkham as master of the *Jolly Bachelor,* loaded a cargo of twenty slaves and sent her back to sea. Although her next destination had probably been the West Indies, the new captain took her straight to America, putting in at Newport, Rhode Island.

Since slaves could be and were sold in the New England colonies at that time, the twenty blacks were easily disposed of for 1,624 pounds and the *Jolly Bachelor* was sold for 1,300 pounds. This was in colonial currency, which was not worth as much as British sterling, but it was enough to repay the factor Burchall's claim against the ship.

Peter Faneuil never learned of the *Jolly Bachelor*'s disastrous voyage. He died suddenly, at the early age of forty-two, before the slaver reached Newport.

The records of slave trading in Connecticut and New Hampshire are scarce. Many historians of such seaports as New Haven, New London, Middletown and Mystic in Connecticut, and Portsmouth and Dover in New Hampshire simply do not mention it at all. But here and there a record can be found indicating that the trade did go on, though to a lesser extent than in Massachusetts and Rhode Island.

There was a great deal of trade from Connecticut ports, as well as other New England ones, direct to the West Indies with the products the New England colonies could supply in return for sugar, molasses, rum and other tropical products. This trade was not as profitable as slaving, but it was far less risky.

One slaver from Upper Middletown (today Cromwell) on the Connecticut River was wrecked on the West African coast. Her master, James Riley, and his crew were captured by Arab traders, enslaved and taken across the Sahara Desert to Morocco. This, at least, seems to be one case where the white men aboard a slaver got what they deserved, and found out what it was like to be slaves.

Another disastrous voyage in the Connecticut slave trade was made in 1764 from New London by the sloop *Adventure*. Her captain, Joseph Miller, and all of his crew except one man died of one of the deadly African diseases while the vessel was trading off Sierra Leone. When an English factor ashore sent two men to take off the *Adventure*'s cargo, black natives boarded the ship, murdered the three still aboard and plundered the cargo.

In 1787 it appeared that some of Connecticut's ports might enjoy a boom, for in that year the Rhode Island legislature passed a law prohibiting the slave trade. This was accomplished by an antislavery group led by none other than one of the famous Brown brothers—Moses, the one who turned Quaker and devoted the rest of his life to abolishing the slave trade. Fines for violating the new law were stiff—100 pounds for each slave carried aboard a Rhode Island slaver, and 1,000 pounds against the vessel making such a voyage in the trade.

The Rhode Island slave-ship owners were indignant, but they thought they saw a way out of their troubles. Neighboring Connecticut had no such law. They decided to fit out and sail the slavers from Norwich, on the Thames River, and Middletown, on the Connecticut.

However, Moses Brown and his followers promptly went to work on the Connecticut legislature and in 1788 that state too outlawed the slave trade.

Public opinion was beginning to turn against slavery and the slave trade. The time was coming when harsh punishments would be enforced against those in the trade if their slavers were captured by United States cruisers. Merchant-ship owners began to look elsewhere for profit—to the China tea trade, the California trade and whaling over the seven seas.

9.

The End of It

No one really knows exactly when the New England Triangular Trade ended, although there were reports of New England slavers landing slaves in Cuba as late as 1862—during the Civil War that was fought to free the slaves in the United States. Some of the New England colonies had passed laws abolishing slavery in those colonies more than two centuries earlier. But it was much later before action was taken to abolish the trade entirely.

In 1641 Massachusetts Bay forbade the importation of slaves into the colony. In 1652 Rhode Island went even further; it not only prohibited the importation of slaves there but also provided that all slaves who had been in the colony ten years, and all who reached the age of twenty-four, should be freed.

Yet little was done to enforce these laws, much less to stop the slave trade itself, and in time the laws were repealed or ignored. Most ships in the Triangular Trade disposed of their human cargoes in the West Indies, but all through the seventeenth and part of the eighteenth century slaves were sometimes brought to New England and sold there. Slavery was legal in all thirteen of the original states of the United States of America when the Declaration of Independence was proclaimed July 4, 1776.

But in the latter part of the eighteenth century, states began abolishing the importation of slaves. Even southern states did so—Virginia in 1778, Maryland in 1783. At about the same time North Carolina placed such a high duty on imported slaves that the effect was the same. South Carolina did not go all the way; in 1787 it forbade the importation of slaves for five years, leaving the door open in case more new slaves were needed from Africa.

All this did nothing to stop the Triangular Trade. New England ships could still take their cargoes of rum to the Guinea Coast, slaves to the West Indies and molasses back to New England.

Great Britain made the first move to abolish the trade. Her ships had been the most numerous and active in slaving, and there were British castles and factories all along the Guinea Coast. But many people in Britain, especially members of various religious organizations, were determined to stop the shameful trade. In 1806 they succeeded, and Parliament passed a law ending all slave trading by British vessels.

A number of American states had already done the same thing, including Massachusetts, Rhode Island and Connecticut, and in 1808 the United States Congress passed a law prohibiting any Americans from participating in the slave trade. But these laws were not really enforced and were winked at by the merchant-ship owners in the trade. It will be remembered that the *Sukey,* in 1802, sailed with a stock of planks and boards in her cargo for "repairs," and that they were not installed as an extra deck for the slaves until the vessel was on the Guinea Coast. A ship sailing to trade in West Africa was doing nothing wrong unless it could be proved she was a slaver. Britain's complete abolishment of the trade meant more gold to line the pockets of Americans operating slavers.

British naval squadrons were sent to patrol the Gulf of Guinea and capture slavers. But America's War of 1812 with Britain put an end to the practice of stopping and searching American vessels. A slaver flying American colors could thumb her nose at a patrol vessel flying the Union Jack of Britain.

The English negotiated treaties with Portugal, Spain, the Netherlands, Sweden and France under which those nations too agreed to give up the slave trade. But many a slaver of these nations that ran afoul of a British cruiser would simply hoist the Stars and Stripes and sail on, for the United States had refused to sign such a treaty with Britain.

At last, however, in 1842, the Webster-Ashburton Treaty between the United States and Britain was signed. It settled certain boundary disputes between the United States and British-held Canada and other matters, including United States cooperation with Britain in ending the slave trade.

After that it was harder for American slave traders, but they were far from beaten. American shipbuilders were expert at turning out sleek, fast vessels. These new ships were called clippers, although they were mostly topsail schooners and brigs, not the swift, full-rigged ships that later became famous on the seas. But they could usually outsail the naval patrols the United States now sent to the Gulf of Guinea.

American efforts there were half-hearted in any case. Between 1843 and 1857 the United States squadrons on the Guinea Coast were never more than seven ships, while the British never had less then twelve. And although American cruisers did make some captures, it was not enough to put a dent in the illegal slave trade.

The market for slaves in the West Indies had been greatly reduced, however. In almost all of them the importing of more slaves had been forbidden. Besides, with children being born into slavery on the islands, there were enough workers for the sugar cane fields.

There was one important exception to this—Spanish-held Cuba. The island, biggest of all in the West Indies, was expanding its sugar cane crop. It still needed slaves and would pay prices for them that kept the gold clinking into New England merchant-ship owners' coffers. In 1847 able-bodied slaves were being sold along the Gold Coast for the ridiculously low price of $10. In Cuba these same slaves would bring as much as $625 each.

It was 1860 before something happened to signal the beginning of the end for the New England Triangular Trade. In that year the *Erie,* built in Warren, Rhode Island, sailed for the Guinea Coast.

Her captain, Nathaniel Gordon, was a "downeaster" from Portland, one of the great breed of Maine seafaring men. He is said to have made three earlier slaving voyages, so he probably knew what he was about.

Indeed, although the vessel was good-sized, he jammed a cargo into the *Erie* that must nearly have made her hull bulge out—890 slaves, including 106 women and 612 children, all loaded near the mouth of the Congo River in West Africa.

Then Captain Gordon headed for the Middle Passage and Cuba. But no sooner had he sailed than his luck ran out. Fast though the *Erie* was, she could not outrun one of the new ships partly driven by steam—the American sloop of war *Mohican*. The *Mohican* captured her, set the slaves free on the coast of Liberia and took the *Erie* to New York, where Captain Gordon was arrested and tried for his life.

His first trial ended with a "hung jury" when the jurors could not decide on a verdict. But the government persisted and brought him to trial again. This time he was found guilty and sentenced to death.

The trial caused a sensation, chiefly because Captain Gordon refused to reveal the names of the *Erie's* owners, who were also liable for the death penalty. They were probably wealthy, respected merchants and they seem to have shown their appreciation of Gordon's silence by using all their influence to save his life. When a rumor spread that a mob was about to storm the jail and rescue Captain Gordon, the government sent a detachment of marines to surround the jail with fixed bayonets.

Preparations were made for Gordon's execution.

But in some way a large dose of strychnine, a powerful poison, was smuggled into the jail and Gordon swallowed it.

As he rolled on the floor in agony, he shouted at his guards, "I've cheated you!"

But the prison doctor managed to save his life, and Gordon went to the gallows. No doubt this caused the owners of the *Erie*, as well as others in the slave trade, to have some sober thoughts. Next time the captain of a captured slaver might not be silent about his owners. . . .

From then on the trade in human flesh dropped off to almost nothing. There was a report in 1862 that a vessel named the *Ocilla* of Mystic, Connecticut, had landed slaves in Cuba. She seems to have been the last of the New England slavers, though according to another rumor a New York vessel did the same in 1864.

The greedy, brutal business was over, but the damage had been done. It would be the middle of the twentieth century before most of the black people of the West Indies, although freed long before, would win their full independence from the European nations that had helped to colonize the islands with slaves from West Africa.

The story of the New England Triangular Trade is a shameful tale of greed and inhumanity. It is not a pretty story, but one that should be told because its repercussions are still being felt today. The legacy that it left—of anger, conflict and mistrust between blacks and whites, both in this country and abroad—remains a major problem to be solved before there can be equality and freedom for all throughout the world.

For Further Reading

Of the more easily obtainable books on this subject, _Black Cargoes,_ by Daniel P. Mannix, is probably the best one covering the West Indies slave trade in general. Also recommended are _Bristol, Rhode Island: A Town Biography_, by Mark Antony De Wolfe Howe, for its material on the deWolf brothers and Bristol's slave trade; James B. Hedges' _The Browns of Providence Plantations_, for the story of that famous family; _Rum, Romance and Rebellion_, by Charles William Taussig—interesting and easy reading; Theodore Canot's _Adventures of an African Slaver_ because of his extensive travels in West Africa in the early nineteenth century; and _Economic and Social History of New England,_ by William B. Weeden, for its excellent discussion and description of the New England slave trade.

Other excellent sources recommended, when available, are: _Black Mother,_ by Basil Davidson; _A Historical Account of St. Thomas, West Indies, and Incidental Notices of St. Croix and St. John,_ by John P. Knox; and two articles in Volume 11, 1926, of the _Journal of Negro History:_ "Account of the Negro Rebellion on St. Croix," by Engelbert Hesselberg, and "Slavery on British West India Plantations," by Frank Wesley Pitman.

Bibliography

ALDERMAN, CLIFFORD LINDSEY. *Wooden Ships and Iron Men.* New York: Walker, 1964.

ATWATER, EDWARD E. *History of New Haven.* New York: W. W. Munsell, 1887.

BLACK, CLINTON V. *The Story of Jamaica.* London: Collins, 1965.

BURNS, ALAN. *The History of the British West Indies.* London: George Allen & Unwin, 1965.

CANOT, THEODORE. *Adventures of an African Slaver.* New York: Dover, 1969.

CARNES, J. A. *Journal of a Voyage from Boston to the West Coast of Africa.* Boston: John P. Jewett, 1852.

CAULKINS, FRANCIS MAINWARING. *History of New London, Connecticut.* New London, Conn.: Published by the author, 1852.

CHANNING, GEORGE G. *Early Recollections of Newport.* Newport, R.I.: A. J. Ward, Charles E. Hammett, Jr., 1868.

DAVIDSON, BASIL. *Black Mother.* Boston: Little, Brown, 1961.

DOW, CHARLES H. *Newport: The City by the Sea.* Newport, R.I.: John P. Sanderson, 1880.

DOW, GEORGE FRANCIS. *Slave Ships and Slaving.* Salem, Mass.: Marine Research Society, 1927.

FELT, JOSEPH B. *Annals of Salem.* Boston: Munroe, 1849.

FOOTE, ANDREW H. *Africa and the American Flag.* New York: D. Appleton, 1862.

GARDNER, W. J. *A History of Jamaica.* New York: D. Appleton, 1909.

GREENE, WELCOME ARNOLD. *The Providence Plantations for 250 Years.* Providence, R.I.: J. A. & R. A. Reid, 1886.

HEDGES, JAMES B. *The Browns of Providence Plantations.* Cambridge, Mass.: Harvard University Press, 1952.

HESSELBERG, ENGELBERT. "Account of the Negro Rebellion on St. Croix." *Journal of Negro History,* Vol. 11, 1926.

HILL, EVERETT C. *A Modern History of New Haven and Eastern New Haven County.* New York: S. J. Clarke, 1918.

HOULETTE, WILLIAM D. "Rum Trading in the American Colonies." *Journal of American History,* Vol. 28, No. 3, 1934.

HOWE, MARK ANTONY DE WOLFE. *Bristol, Rhode Island: A Town Biography.* Cambridge, Mass.: Harvard University Press, 1930.

KNOX, JOHN P. *A Historical Account of St. Thomas, West Indies, and Incidental Notices of St. Croix and St. John.* New York: Scribner, 1852.

MAKINSON, DAVID H. *Barbados: A Study of North American-West Indian Relations, 1739–1789.* London: Mouton, 1964.

MANNIX, DANIEL P. *Black Cargoes.* New York: Viking, 1965.

MARSHALL, BENJAMIN TINKER (editor). *A Modern History of New London County.* New York: Lewis, 1922.

MAY, RALPH. *Early Portsmouth History.* Boston: C. E. Goodspeed, 1926.

MILLER, JOHN C. *Origins of the American Revolution.* Boston: Little, Brown, 1943.

MOORE, GEORGE H. *Notes on the History of Slavery in Massachusetts.* New York: D. Appleton, 1865.

MUNRO, WILFRED H. *The History of Bristol.* Providence, R.I.: J. A. & R. A. Reid, 1880.

OSGOOD, CHARLES S., AND BATCHELDER, H. M. *Historical Sketch of Salem.* Salem, Mass.: Essex Institute, 1879.

OSTERWEIS, ROLLIN G. *Three Centuries of New Haven.* New Haven: Yale University Press, 1953.

PARK, MUNGO. *Travels in the Interior Parts of Africa.* London: W. Bulmer, 1799.

PHILLIPS, JAMES DUNCAN. *Salem in the Eighteenth Century.* Boston: Houghton Mifflin, 1937.

PITMAN, FRANK WESLEY. "Slavery on British West India Plantations." *Journal of Negro History,* Vol. 11, 1926.

POYER, JOHN. *The History of Barbados, 1605 to 1801.* London: J. Mawman, 1808.

ROBERTS, W. ADOLPHE. *The Caribbean.* New York: Bobbs-Merrill, 1940.

——. *The French in the West Indies.* New York: Bobbs-Merrill, 1942.

SHEA, MARGARET M. *The Story of Colonial Newport.* Newport, R.I.: Published by the author, 1912.

SMITH, G. H. "Cruelties of West India Slavery at the Moment." London: *The Morning Chronicle,* Oct. 8, 1829.

TAUSSIG, CHARLES WILLIAM. *Rum, Romance and Rebellion.* New York: Minton, Balch, 1928.

WEEDEN, WILLIAM B. *Economic and Social History of New England.* New York: Hillary House, 1963.

WINSLOW, OLA ELIZABETH. *Portsmouth: The Life of a Town.* New York: Macmillan, 1966.

Index